LAST ONE IN

LAST ONE IN

Tales of a New England Boyhood

John Gould

with illustrations by F. Wenderoth Saunders

Camden, Maine

Published by Down East Books
An imprint of The Rowman & Littlefield Publishing Group, Inc.
4501 Forbes Boulevard, Suite 200, Lanham, Maryland 20706
www.rowman.com

Unit A, Whitacre Mews, 26-34 Stannary Street, London SE11 4AB, United Kingdom

Distributed by NATIONAL BOOK NETWORK

Library of Congress Cataloging-in-Publication Data is available on file

Library of Congress Control Number: 66022675

ISBN: 978-1-60893-550-5 (pbk. : alk. paper)
ISBN: 978-1-60893-551-2 (electronic)

♾™ The paper used in this publication meets the minimum requirements of American National Standard for Information Sciences—Permanence of Paper for Printed Library Materials, ANSI/NISO Z39.48-1992.

Printed in the United States of America

FOR WILLY

In your grandfather's time there was more "progress" than in any other equal time in history. This was not altogether his fault. In my grandfather's boyhood he went with a horse and buggy, and when he was an old man he still went with a horse and buggy. In my lifetime I rode with him behind his horse, and about the time you were born I sat in my chair in Maine and watched them send up astronauts in Florida. When I was a boy two dozen steam trains a day went through town, but you can't ride on a steam train because there aren't any more. So I thought I'd ramble along a little, so there'd be someplace for you to look and see what you missed by one lifetime. Love you!

GRAMPIE JOHN

THE TESTIMONIAL:

I have read this manuscript, and dare say it will be best appreciated by intelligent people.

PETER PARTOUT
Peppermint Corner

LAST ONE IN

THE THREE BIRDIES

No birdie with a yellow bill ever hopped upon my windowsill, cocked his shining eye and said, "Ain't you 'shamed, you sleepy-head!" Waking up, for me, in my down-Maine attic room with the faded, forlorn wallpaper roses, was Grampie Nugent, Secretary Potter and Whisperin' Gleason. We had birds, but those three got up before the birds.

Secretary Potter wasn't a secretary to anything. He got the title from John B. Manchester, who had inherited three seafaring fortunes which he invested wisely and consequently was not a man to clean out his own backhouse. Our Down East coastal community had no public sewers then, and a backhouse was an unfunny necessity that required occasional laundering. This wasn't a job people ran around looking for, and any useful citizen who would oblige was much in demand. Potter was available, although his major profession was housekeeping at Harry Dunbar's livery stable. Mr. Manchester had asked Potter to perform and he was now under the end of the barn performing. Mr. Manchester was at a discreet distance, sitting on the top strake of the whitewashed barnyard fence, superintending the labor, when Mrs. Manchester stepped out of the house to toss a few table scraps to the White Wyandottes. "Who's that?" she asked, with natural interest in the identity of such a contractor, and Mr. Manchester said, "I'm giving a little dictation to my secretary." It stuck, and ever afterwards he was Secretary Potter.

About five-thirty every morning in summer, Secretary Potter would open the big rolling doors on the livery stable and sweep out with a rattan barn broom. The wheels on the doors had never tasted oil, so they set up a protest that cringed the whole village and fetched up against my faded wallpaper roses to bring an end to sleep. Morning, birds or not, had come.

My second alarm clock, had I needed one, was Grampie Nugent. He pushed a wheelbarrow to the village every morning and greeted everybody along the way with his high, squeaky voice — a voice

4

tuned to the squeal of his ungreased wheelbarrow wheel. He never bought so much that he needed a wheelbarrow, but it went where he did. From my room I could hear him when he cleared the Baptist church on Main Street, where he said good morning to Jack Randall. Then he would say good morning to Guy Soule, to Fred Moulton, to Cap'n Jule Soule, to Edgar Conant, to Mrs. Luce — and at last to Whisperin' Gleason.

This took him almost to the village, and Whisperin' Gleason would fall into step beside Grampie Nugent and walk along as far as the livery stable, where he trained some broken-down trotting horses not yet written off. Whisperin' Gleason was called Whisperin' for the same reason we called bald-headed Joe Ramsay Curly, and six-foot-six Lester Glover Shorty. His good morning to Grampie Nugent was a burst of cannonade. Even when he imparted the most secret thing you could hear him all over town. For a hundred yards Grampie Nugent and Whisperin' Gleason would talk along — discussing such things as the prospect of showers, the shortage of good hay, and always the state of Grampie's health. He was having trouble holding his water, and the personal and intimate details of this distress came to me in my bedroom and were interesting. When I heard Whisperin' Gleason greet Secretary Potter I knew they had reached the livery stable, and the day had begun.

One day a year, at planting time, Grampie Nugent would leave his wheelbarrow home and take his garden hoe to town. Beginning at the Universalist

5

church we had a cement sidewalk that ran all the way to the "corner," which is what we called the village. It was the only paving in town, and it offered Grampie a grindstone he didn't have to turn. He would drag the hoe along behind him and the concrete would hone it to a wonderful edge for murdering weeds. There is nothing a birdie on a windowsill could ever sing to equal a hoe dragged through town on a cement sidewalk. On the mornings he did this the racket drowned out his greetings to Jack Randall, Guy Soule, Fred Moulton, Cap'n Jule and Mrs. Luce.

But not Whisperin' Gleason. Nothing drowned him out.

Every morning of my growing up began in that attic bedroom. It had no heat in it, and I was mostly grown before we ran up a wire and had an electric light. I had a stand for my kerosene lamp, but mostly I would undress in the dark. I could see the lights of the village from my window, and millions of stars. The four-pane frame didn't go up or down, but it would lift out entirely and I usually slept with it out, winter and summer. I was taught to believe in fresh air. When the wind hauled southerly and we had a slashing warm rain, or when a bitter no'theast blizzard whipped biting snow, I left the window in. There were hot nights and cold nights and not much in between, but mostly it was a wonderful place to sleep. The rain would slant against the roof faster than it would run off sometimes, and it was a lullaby kings couldn't hire. In winter driving snowflakes would seem to be wearing the crisp cedar shingles away, and the rafters would creak in the wind. Here I kept the private souvenirs of my youth, and good comforters for subzero nights. When it was cold I would jump up in the morning and dress fast, pulling on the clothing that had been cooling for me all night, and I would hurry down to the kitchen. I didn't hurry like that when it was summertime.

In summertime, when Secretary Potter opened the doors and made ready for the influx of horse-hiring drummers who would come on the 7:18 train, waking up in my room was joyful. I could tell exactly what time it was by looking to see which faded rose was fairest in the newborn sun. As the year revolved, the roses brightened and dimmed with the angle of the dawn. When I had the measles I counted the roses on my walls, and there were one thousand four hundred and eighty. I had to move the bureau to count behind it, and I was too weak to push it back — so Mother thought I must have been delirious. When the sun got over to the row of roses by the bookcase it was August, and that was the best time of all. The Minister Apples were ready, and those that fell during the night were mine. They were Strawberry St. Lawrence apples, really, but my father observed they were pretty to look at but mealy to take and he called them the Minister Apples. I never thought them mealy. I didn't wear much in

7

August, so it didn't take long to dress and get out to pick up Minister Apples before the hens and birds got to them.

Through the house and the kitchen, through the shed and the barn, and out the back barn door I would run, and the dew on the grass was suddenly cool and beautiful on my bare feet. Dew on bare feet on a bright August morning is the greatest diuretic of all, so I would pause, feet wide apart, and my best shot was about eight feet, freehand. I killed all the grass outside the back barn door, until my father told me to find a new place or we'd be living in a desert.

In wintertime waking up was to the bells. Somebody would tingle a cutter down the main street with the little shaker bells ringle-jingling, or a heavy team would go by with the matched, mellowed, steel melody that muted itself in the frosty air. No two teams had the same bells, and I could tell from my bed if 'twere Merle Prout or Bess Means, or sometimes George Bartol bringing an early load of pressed hay to the team track for the police horses in Boston. He had that contract sewed up, and loaded cars off and on all winter, and his team had a peal of bells that was majestic. I was almost through high school when one morning was massacred by a new and hateful sound — George Bartol had bought a tractor! It snorted its way to the railroad, and he could make bigger loads and go faster. Whisperin' Gleason said, "B'Gawd, Bartol, when everybody has them things, what's to haul hay to?"

If the night had snowed, the team bells in the morning would be Milt Dill's. Milt teamed for Edgar Conant, who had the town contract to break roads. In those days he who broke least broke best, because every farmer in town had sleds. Edgar just shoved a timber through the stays of his logging runners, and Milt would drive around. It packed the snow down some, and smoothed it a little. It would still be hip-deep to us short-legged youngsters when we wallowed to school, but we were thankful for Milt. Without him, the going would be tough.

Summertime was warmer, but it was no prettier. I used the backhouse in the barn in winter, and didn't dally around. I could look out the back barn windows and see my Minister Apple tree dark against the snow, and beyond it the black spruce woods. No apples now, but under the spruces would be fat rabbits to make hot pies with crunchy crusts, and pa'tridges would be coming from under the new snow to sit on limbs and wait for me. Not on weekdays — after-school time was too short. But on Saturdays I would give things my attention. So when the morning brightened my attic window, summer or winter, a whole world was out there inviting my attention — to do with as I chose. I just had to get up first, and except for measles and mumps and things like that I did. I never missed much.

THE LONE SCOUT

IF we stayed around to watch the racehorses too long Secretary Potter would try to think of something for us to do. He never kicked us out, but there were times he suggested hard. This was before any attempts at organized recreation, and we were too early to embrace any program of the President's Council on Physical Fitness. Then the Boy Scouts of America appeared on the scene and offered us some relief from the boredom of our own company. Secretary Potter thought this might keep us from underfoot, too, so he strongly urged us all to sign up. We did, but the Boy Scouts were ahead of their time with us, and the movement failed. In spite of Secretary Potter's ardent support, they lasted about three weeks.

We gave the Boy Scouts a fair try, though. The movement was new then, and the first we heard of it was when Gooky Griffin began acting odd. He was one of us, but suddenly he left off, and after a while we found out it was because he got a magazine for

Christmas. Some aunt had sent him this magazine, and it was the official publication of the Lone Scouts. When the Boy Scouts began to be important some smart printer got a bright idea, and he invented this "lone" scout substitute. If you were a boy away off by yourself and there was no Boy Scout troop for you to belong to, you could become a Lone Scout all by yourself, and still derive all the benefits of the movement. You found out how to be a Lone Scout by taking this magazine, and you could write in and buy the uniform, badges and all the rest. Thus Gooky became a Lone Scout and didn't play with the rest of us any more. We'd see him skulking off by himself, keeping an eye on us from afar and warning us of pitfalls and dangers, whether they existed or not, and before we found out that he had become a Lone Scout we thought he had gone crazy. He used to leave us notes in cleft sticks saying, "Beware!" When we did find out about it, we let him go it.

But about that time somebody came to town from the Boy Scouts of America, and the Men's Brotherhood at the church agreed to sponsor a troop. As soon as word ran around, Secretary Potter and Whisperin' Gleason became the hottest advocates of this, although neither belonged to the Brotherhood. Thanks mostly to them, we turned out twenty-seven boys at the church vestry for the organization meeting, and we became Boy Scouts.

It was the knots that put our Boy Scout troop on the skids. This man came from headquarters for the first few meetings, and about the second time he showed us how to tie knots. He had a hank of sash-cord and he would cut off a length, tie a knot, and tack it on a board with the name written under-neath. He made the mistake of teaching knots to a couple-dozen boys who knew more about knots than he did. When he made a bowline we could all see that it was something he planned to tack on a board, and that he had no idea what a bowline is used for in the great wide world outside of church vestries. When he made a bowline he didn't "put his arse be-hind him" — a manner of speaking that has probably never been accepted in the formal rituals of the Boy Scouts of America, but a bowline requirement drilled into us by every sea captain in town. From the time we were knee-high to a scupper and had made our first attempt at securing a skiff, those old mariners had said, "No, Sonny, not like that — here, let me show you!" And when you've been shown, like that, you always do it the right way, forever and ever.

The Boy Scouts didn't know our lingo. Aboard ship there were, oddly enough, only a few ropes. The bellrope, the handrope, the footrope, the manrope, and a few others. But then you didn't use ropes for other things. You had lines, stays, halyards, sheets — and you bent and belayed. And every skipper had told every boy that any fool could tie a knot — the test came in untying it. The man from the Boy Scouts showed us the "square knot" and he tacked it on the board without one word about taking it apart again. But we all knew that was a reefknot and that a sailor aloft could jerk it with one hand and let the sail go. The same with a bowline — no matter how much strain you put to it, it eases itself with a simple twist. And the clove hitch. That isn't really a knot at all, but it will hold anything, and then slips free in a twinkling if you want line. That evening we all saw that the Boy Scouts were on the wrong end of the business — the man never untied one knot all evening. We went home.

Then there was a meeting to plan a hike. Secretary Potter said, "A hike!" Grover Kendall had agreed to be our scoutmaster, and to that Secretary Potter said, "My, my!" Grover was a mild-mannered old maid of a fellow who was considered harmless, and his professional career was putting covers on pasteboard shoe boxes in the shipping room at the moccasin factory. He did this job faithfully and with unerring accuracy, and it was said the factory couldn't operate without him, as nobody else in town was stupid enough to do it. It was what we called idiot's work. So Grover agreed to be our leader and he studied the manual so our first hike would be a big success. We would study how to make trails, select campsites, build fireplaces and fires, cook, and all the things that would win us badges. Grover said the best thing for a hike was to take plenty of fresh milk, and we all looked at each other. Scattered throughout the woodlands of our community, and in the clefts of rocks alongshore, were our coffee pots. We boys picked them up regularly on Saturday mornings at the stores, because they were the gallon tins the shucked oysters came in for the Friday trade. The storekeepers all kept them for us. Whenever we tried out a new campsite we'd leave an oyster can upside down so it would be there for the next time. They'd last a summer, but winter would rust them. When half filled with water and brought to a rolling boil with a couple of handfuls of ground coffee, they'd decant a thick, rank, sturdy beverage that adequately took the place of milk. Neither did we rally to Grover's menu of frankfurters to be cooked on a stick. Our own untutored fireside meals of fish chowders, fried rabbit, baked salmon and hot biscuits were quite all we really wanted. Suddenly the Boy Scout program seemed unsophisticated. Merton Chalmers raised his hand and said he didn't care for frankfurters.

But we went on the hike. We met at the church instead of our usual rendezvous known secretly amongst ourselves as "No. 4." With Grover Kendall on ahead carrying the Boy Scout manual and a ten-quart dairy can of nice milk we paraded up Main Street before the goggling eyes of the townspeople, including Secretary Potter and Whisperin' Gleason, feeling silly, and we turned in at the sawmill and headed for the woods. Grover showed us how to snap the ends on branches so we could find our way home again, and didn't seem to know that we raced this same route every warm evening after school, spring and fall, to jump into the pool of Stacy's Brook. Grover had told us all to bring our bathing suits because we might take what the manual called a "dip," but none of us had brought one. We didn't own any. Some of the girls used to go swimming with us in Stacy's Brook, too, and they used to wear the same kind of suit we did. Well, not quite.

After Grover read us the part about selecting a campsite we came to our No. 7, which was at the big ledge by the spring, and after he read to us about building a fireplace we used the fireplace we'd had there for years. He read the instructions about building a fire, and while he was reading Mert Chalmers poured some kerodust from his bottle, pulled a match dipped in paraffin from his capband, and got a fire going. Kerodust is sawdust with kerosene, and a spoonful of it will start a fire with wet wood in a no'theast rainstorm. We all had a bottle of it, ready to go. Then Mert mixed up his biscuits and got some water going for a bullbeef stew, and while he was doing it Grover read us the section about passing a Boy Scout cooking test. It was very interesting.

Then we found out that Gooky Griffin was scouting us, and had left a note in a bottle that some blueberries were ripe on Big Knoll. This was excellent intelligence and we all went over and picked blueberries while Mert went home to get an egg so he could convert his biscuits to a blueberry cake. He took the shortcut through Loring's pasture, so he wasn't gone very long. Our first Boy Scout hike consisted of Grover Kendall's standing by a tree reading from a book, and the rest of us doing what we did on any good Saturday anyway.

We went to a few more Boy Scout meetings after

that, but the attendance thinned down. When we were asked to spend money for uniforms and a flag we bowed out. The man who tied knots came from headquarters to whip our enthusiasm back, but he gave up. Even Secretary Potter and Whisperin' Gleason had luked off. The only boy in our time who ever got to be a good scout was Gooky Griffin, and he took the magazine for a couple of years and enjoyed it. The Lone Scout signal was the cry of the wild turkey gobbler. Only another Lone Scout would know what it meant. Gooky would be off by himself, the only living Lone Scout around, and he would let go with the cry of the wild turkey gobbler. It sounded just fine. We never answered him, because we were not Lone Scouts and we were not turkey gobblers. There were no wild turkeys in our countryside, so we always knew exactly where Gooky was.

THE SULPHURED OATS

A BOY's will was the wind's will, and if we didn't overstay we were welcome about anywhere we went. Some good stories look upon the post office and the general store as the heartbeat of the village, but I'm going to bet on the livery stable. Mothers didn't always like to have us hanging around the place, but the genteel trading and trafficking of the store and post office couldn't hold a candle to breeding a mare in Harry Dunbar's. A rich culture awaited the eager student there, and this included the seventeen origins of profanity as expounded by Whisperin' Gleason. Hardly anything took place in town that didn't begin or end at the livery stable, at least to the extent of solid opinions. And it wasn't always uncouth — Harry Dunbar himself was a model of propriety and looked as if he might be a retired Presbyterian preacher. He was, indeed, a past Grand Master of the Masons, and as a Mark Mason had entered his trade as "Equine Custodian, Stabulator and

Entrepreneur." He rented horses and rigs, stabled them for folks who didn't want the care of their own animals, and provided comfort for the broken-down trotting nags our sporting set had a flair for accumulating.

Secretary Potter was his Left-hand Man, as he put it, and Potter always knew everything that was going on, whether it was true or not. His day began by feeding and grooming the animals, and getting five or six ready for the salesmen who would hop off the morning train. These salesmen, called drummers, would make their calls and return the rigs before the evening train to the next town. Most of them came on schedule and preferred certain horses and buggies. Potter knew which was which. He also had to keep one horse always ready, day and night, for Dr. Gilchrist, and if a call came at two o'clock in the morning Secretary could get the doctor on his way quicker than you'd believe. If we heard those big doors squeal open on their rusty rollers during the night we could guess about who was having a baby.

Secretary Potter was not above a jest, and if somebody wanted a rig to take a lady riding it was just like him to slip a dose of sulphured oats to the horse beforehand. This sets up an amusing reaction, although a horse that toots o'er hill and dale with every step is not the best accompaniment for the sweet nothings of a romance. Some would wait to see which horse Secretary hitched in, and then ask for another one. Secretary would protest that his choice was clever, but when he got caught up on it he'd shift horses with a grin. He pulled the sulphur trick on a salesman who decided to stay over and woo a girl up at Maple Corner, and when the salesman brought the horse back he beat Secretary up. Really did a job on him.

Whisperin' Gleason didn't work for Harry Dunbar but he was always around the stable, and he picked up some kind of a living training and driving racehorses. Depending on whether an owner wanted to win or lose, he'd let Gleason drive. He could do either. Except for an occasional boy who was handed a nickel for sweeping up or washing a buggy, this completed the livery stable roster except for Mort Hudson, who had a Morris chair just inside the big doors and would sit there on good days to see everything. Mort was old, but still sharp as a tack, and city people would have taken him for the town sage. His big amusement was to ask questions. Mostly he'd say, "Think they'll have it?"

Try this out on today's market. Today ten out of ten will answer, "Have what?" But if any of us boys had come up with anything as thin as that Mort would rack us up as a poor risk and remark that our father didn't get his seed back. He always liked one answer I gave him: "They can't — the font froze." Toady Barnes, who wasn't supposed to be all there, always gave the same answer: "They had it yestiddy." Chuck Lambert used to say, "They come and borried my rope." A good reply was "I sold my ten tickets." Or "We got the lunch packed." The standard answer was "The tents are up!" But everybody was supposed to have an answer for Mort's questions, and this was an intellectual challenge because all he had to do was sit there and think them up, and we always shot from the hip. One day I had two cents and was going to Magoon's store to get Mother a yeast cake, and I popped into the livery stable to bring myself up to date, and old Mort greeted me with, "Have you got Tidy Bibber's spats?"

Tidy was called tidy because he wasn't, and spats were funny to us whether we linked them with Tidy or not. Secretary Potter leaned on his broom to hear what I would say.

I said, "Just the red ones."

The look Mort gave me was a greater honor than a Ph.D. from Harvard. He approved. He told about it all day. "He sure topped me that time! 'Just the red ones,' he says. Har, har, har!"

One Saturday morning in October, I went into the livery stable and Secretary Potter had a job for me. We'd had six inches of wet snow the night before, and at daybreak he'd sent Dr. Gilchrist on a baby case over on Beech Hill with a sleigh. The sun had come up, the wind had shifted and the day was warm. By eight o'clock the snow was gone. Secretary had to go and get the doctor, and he had one horse hitched into a wagon and another into a buggy. I drove the wagon for him, and he followed behind. When we got to the place the doctor was still busy, so we shifted the hitching weight and left him the buggy. We boosted the sleigh into the wagon, tied the sleigh-horse to the tailgate, and came back to town. The spare horse had a bellyband of jingle bells, and he tinkled just fine when we trotted up the street, and I was glad that people took notice of me while I was performing this great public service. Secretary Potter said, "I'd pay you well, but you'd just go and spend it." But Harry Dunbar gave me a dime which, of course, I went and spent just as Secretary had said.

Harry had a couple of stallions, and from time to time the livery stable was an arena of wild confusion. Whisperin' Gleason always officiated at these functions and after he made a few introductory remarks everybody in town knew what was going on. When he yelled at Secretary Potter, "Hold her tail up, you damn fool!" the crowd would gather. It was generally believed that breeding a mare would proceed more smoothly if left to the horses, but the participation of Potter and Gleason swelled the attendance. Service at Harry Dunbar's was a public social event. The last time they tried to breed Muriel W there was some talk about indelicacy, but it was the only time I ever heard adverse comments.

Ned Cushing owned Muriel W at that time, and kept her in a shed at his house up on Laurel Street. She held seven world's records, and her colts always brought a good price. But now she was senile and doubts were entertained. Some said she could be bred again and some said she couldn't. Ned loved her and spent a good while every day exercising her. He would go out on cold nights to see that her blanket was secure, and if she didn't seem happy he would read *Black Beauty* to her and rub her with liniment. He dreaded the day he would have to lay her away. Ned had given up all hopes of breeding her again, himself, but the experts at the livery stable kept telling him he should try again. One solution, they felt, might be a younger stallion. When Harry Dunbar acquired such a stallion Ned agreed, and he led Muriel W down one morning. The usual preparations for the rites were completed. People heard Whisperin' Gleason and assembled.

Nobody, including Muriel W, was sure that Muriel W was ready. She seemed reluctant. This caused Whisperin' Gleason to encourage her, which in turn attracted more people, and finally many were standing outside who couldn't get in. Every day or so, after that, they would bring Muriel W down again to see if her cycle had advanced, and everybody would collect again to see if anything happened. Everybody was ready, and the stallion was ready, but Muriel W wasn't interested. Ned would lead her home and rub her with liniment. She never had another foal. And the poor stallion lost interest in his trade. Whenever they introduced him to a mare he would hang his head and think about Muriel W, and he was sad. Harry finally had to sell him.

Once in a while a keen horse-swap would be going on, or some other business of great privacy, and they'd shoo us boys out. But that was rare, and most of the time we were free to stay. We were expected to jump up and hold a bridle while a horse got harnessed, and lend a hand when we could. If we stayed away for a couple of days, occupied with affairs elsewhere, when we came back Secretary Potter would say, "Where you been? I missed you." A boy growing up likes to hear things like that. It made us feel good. Nobody likes to be counted out, and at Harry Dunbar's livery stable they always counted the boys in.

THE SPARK COIL

IF'N I were to make one dominant criticism of life today, it would be that nobody is amazed any more at anything. We have surmounted so many things, and performed so many miracles, that everything is matter-of-course. This is a great pity. I used to wake up every morning in my attic room ready to be amazed all day long at all manner of things, and I usually was. There was a great deal nobody had discovered and nobody had got used to yet. Today they send television pictures back from the moon and everybody says yes-yes, but I can remember how amazed I was to learn a water pipe would send messages. One time I made Charlie Hawes's sister jump four feet in the air and scream so she was heard in Baltimore, and I did it over a water pipe.

Well, Marconi had done some preliminary work, but he left a great deal to figure out, and Charlie Hawes and I were still monkeying with Sam Morse's telegraph. We connected our respective bedrooms and were having a lot of fun. It was a lot of work stringing a wire so our parents didn't know about it, but we had one strung on bushes and trees, skirting the houses in between, and we used the town water system for the other side of the line. If my folks had known I had grounded some dry cells to the bathroom hopper they might have been fearful, because electricity was a respected thing, but they didn't know it. We kept our telegraph a secret for a long time.

We had to learn the code, but that didn't take long, and then we found we didn't have much to say. We'd sit in school all day thinking about our wonderful telegraph system, and the minute we got out we'd rush home and hitch up the batteries and get ready to send messages. Charlie would tap out, "It is raining here." Then I would answer, "It is raining here, too." "How are you?" he would say, and I would reply, "I am fine, how are things there?" Then he would send, "It is still raining here." This helped our spelling, no doubt, but it wasn't hilarious amusement, and it began to pall. Then we found out we could use the telegraph to surprise people.

Charlie lived three houses down the street, and he would see a woman in a red coat walking by. So he would send me a message: "Woman in red coat coming." Then I would go downstairs and saunter into the kitchen and say to my mother, "I wonder who the woman is in the red coat coming up the street?" Mother would look out the window and there was nobody there, but as she looked this woman in the red coat would come by the house next below and my mother would say, "How did you know she was coming?" But this kind of fun depended on somebody's going by, and in the short evenings after cold weather it depended on being able to see. Then Charlie had the wonderful idea of shocking his sister.

Secretary Potter had given me a spark coil from a Model T. He had entertained the idea of rigging it on Mort Hudson's Morris chair to give the old boy a shock, but he knew Harry Dunbar would cream him if he did, so to put the thing past temptation he gave it to me, and explained how it worked. The ignition system on a Model T included four spark coils under the dashboard, and in the magneto circuit they imparted the wallop that fired the plugs in sequence. You could also hook one of these coils to a dry cell and get the same kind of a wallop for other purposes. Two wires spaced just right in the upholstery of a chair would do fine. Charlie thought his sister would make a wonderful recipient.

I didn't like her anyway, and Charlie didn't, either. She had a boyfriend from the next town who was studying to be a dentist down in Baltimore, and every Friday evening he would call her on the telephone right after supper. She used to two-time him, and she'd be sitting on the little petit point hassock in the front hall talking to him and looking down the street at the same time to see if her date for that night was coming. Charlie fixed things up for the big event, and ran two wires into the petit point so they fitted right in a rosebud and couldn't be seen. He had the spark coil under a window seat, and carefully hid all the wires. Two wires went up to his room and hooked into our telegraph set. Timing was of the essence, so we ran some tests. Charlie would alert me, and then hook up the spark coil. I would count ten seconds — one chimpanzeeses, two chimpanzeeses, three chimpanzeeses . . . — and then I would hold down the key. The Friday evening came when we were ready.

When the telephone rang Charlie kited to his room and gave me the alert. Then he rushed back to the dining room and stood alongside his mother, showing her a smooth piece of pine he thought would make a good model sloop, and setting himself up as an innocent. I counted the required number of chimpanzeeses and depressed the key. On the way to school next morning Charlie told me the thing was a total success, and Mabel went straight up in the air. Charlie's mother, at Mabel's scream, had done a reflex and had swiped Charlie with a handful of dirty dishes, and Charlie's father had leaped up and stood on the dog. But these unforeseen refinements had only made it better, and gave Charlie ample confusion in which to remove the wires from the petit point and destroy telltale evidence. Mabel tended to accuse Charlie, but his mother said, "Charlie was standing right beside me, he didn't do anything!" Charlie said about an hour later Chauncey called back from Baltimore and wanted to know what in the world had cut him off, and what the screaming was about. But Mabel had gone out with Buster Bibber.

But we never got the use out of our telegraph that we expected, and one day I heard my mother say to Dad, "There's some kind of a wire behind the flush," and once they knew about our telegraph the fun was gone. Why we didn't pursue this into the era of radio I can't say. We did find out that the spark coil was a broadcasting station, and we were lucky we never got caught at it. In those days you didn't buy a radio set — you wound coils and made one. The audio tube was yet to come, and there were only a few sending stations on the air. If you had a radio it was a hobby-thing laid out on a long board, and you diddled it patiently to catch feeble signals from Amrad, KDKA, WGY and on sharp, cold nights from the Edgewater Beach Hotel in Chicago. The first manufactured radio set I remember was an Atwater-Kent with headphones, and it was on a long board, too. So whenever anybody made a radio people would come in and listen to it, and they'd sit in rapt silence for hours sometimes, hoping to hear more than a squeal and a squawk. They were readily amazed at any tinkle of music or the suggestion of a voice. If the man had three headphones six people would sit listening at a half apiece. Each dial had to be tenderly adjusted, the cat's whisker had to sit just so on the crystal, and patience and luck would sometimes pay off. It was all very marvelous.

Charlie and I found a good rousing spark off our

coil would register on any radio in town. We didn't even have to be close. These people would be sitting there silently hopeful, and all at once we'd bark their ears off. Since we knew code, we could spice up the context if anybody was able to read us. Everybody would blame the owner of the set for playing a trick on them, and he would exhaust himself denying it. For a year or so Charlie and I were called "local interference" by the radio buffs in town, but we went out of business before anybody discovered us and killed us. There were other things to be amazed at, and we allowed our interests to wander off. There was always something else, and that is a good thing.

THE LAUNCHING

WHEN all the accomplishments of man have been laid end to end, and the last space capsule has probed the last dark foot of infinity, the Final Judgment will probably select the Down East sailing vessel as the fairest deed of all. Not the summer complaint's yawl, or the cup contender, but the real merchant ship intended to make money on the long outside haul. The trim, graceful hulls built from hillside timbers and the high tight sails in wind. On a cold February morning, when I was a boy, I stood in freezing slush on the afterdeck of the *Sintram,* the last big sailing vessel ever built in Maine, and rode her down the ways into the tide. I froze by inches that day, but if somebody told me I might do it again now, I would go and freeze again. I thought the *Sintram* was the finest single accomplishment of the whole twentieth century.

When the *Sintram* slid overboard, a snubline parted and she drifted across the harbor onto the clamflat mud of Wolf's Neck, there to stay for two days until a tug came from Portland to pull her off. But no matter — she was a beautiful vessel and if this was an omen we paid no attention then.

Ours was a shipbuilding and seafaring town. The day of the last Down Easters had gone, but men who built them and sailed them were still around. When you go into our town library you can turn and look up at the working model of the *Dash*. It's a hawk-nest model, and only a suspicion of the fore-and-aft battens are left. But historians come and look at it, and it was always a thrill as a boy to stand and look at the last mortal remains of so famous a ship. She was launched in our town in 1813, built for the Porters of Portland in Master Brewer's yard. I went to school with Brewers, and children still go to school with Brewers there. There are always Brewers. The *Dash* was rigged as a topsail schooner and was fitted for sixteen guns. But after a trial cruise the Porters felt she could stand more sail, so they re-rigged her as a hermaphrodite brig — square forward and schooner aft — and off her main boom they gave her a ringtail. One of our teachers in school told us one time that a "ringtailed peeler" was a follower of Sir Robert Peel in British politics, but old men sitting in the sun gave us the idea he was somebody who peeled a ringtail, so you can take your pick. On the *Dash* the ringtail added a full third to the spread of her canvas, and what the *Dash* did to the British indicates that they weren't familiar with such. In seven cruises, under four skippers, the *Dash* sent in fifteen prizes — all British, all rich, all salable and all profitable. The *Dash* never suffered defeat, never attacked in vain, was never harmed by hostile shot, and knew no equal in speed. Young Cap'n Porter, a bridegroom and but twenty-four years old, took the *Dash* to sea once more, out for one more prize, with a crew of sixty boys from my town, and she was never heard from again. Some thought she foundered on George's Banks. That was a hundred years before my time, but we memorized "The Dead Ship of Harpswell" by Whittier and recited it in school, and we knew he meant our *Dash*.

And hundreds of other ships throughout the long years. When they launched the *John A. Briggs* the President himself came to see, and so did ten thousand other people, and the party went on for days. Cap'n Randall took the *Briggs* to China seas, and his wife went with him, so their children were born in far places. We could see these foreign-born natives walking our streets, and they spoke to us when we passed. But it had been a long time now since the harbormaster's gun had saluted the coming and going of ships, and tools were dull in locked chests. Then came the World War.

As usual, old Uncle Sam was caught flat-footed, and he raced around like a moth in a mitten trying to find a way out. His cry went up for ships, and our town went to building those Ferris-type steamers for the Emergency Fleet. They were wooden, from stock blueprints supplied from Washington, and by our standards were about as seaworthy as a squash, and twice as pretty. But they were wooden ships, and that was our trade. The oldtimers honed their tools and went back to work. We turned out quite a few of these monstrosities before the war subsided, and when the Kaiser gave up we had an unfinished hull on the ways. She was just far enough along so Mrs. Wilson had thought up a name. For some reason the naming of these vessels had been a chore of the President's wife, and she'd send up names that almost made our old shipwrights throw up. There was traditional beauty and dignity and charm to naming a ship, and you had to think a long time. You didn't want a ship ashamed of her name. But whatever the name was that Mrs. Wilson invented, it never got used. The war was over. Orders came to stop work on the hull.

What happened then was utterly foolish, but understandable. We were sailors and shipcrafters, and we loved the sea. Some of the men in town put up money to finish the hull, and they gave Uncle Sam his legal dollar for all rights and title. Then they laid the Ferris-type blueprints out on a trestle-board, and they made rude yellow marks all over them with a crayon. They shoved the stem forward into a rakish taunt and retimbered the bow for cleavage and grace. The ugly stern was rounded off so you could feel the curve and caress the shape with your hand. They shoved things up to get more cargo space, but they tightened the lines so she'd sail. Most important of all, they yanked out the gorming sternposts for the screws, threw the engine beds over the bank, and stepped five lovely masts into the yearning keel. Then they named her the *Sintram*. Once long ago we had built another *Sintram,* and she'd made her way and it was good to remember her in this manner. Everybody said it was wonderful to see sticks in the shipyard again, and nobody took the slightest notice that the world was moving into its own bright future where five-masted schooners would find the sledding hard. Now and then while they were finishing the *Sintram* an airplane would go over — we called them flying machines — and we would look up and marvel that they worked at all. We wondered if they'd ever amount to anything.

A launching was always held on the high-water slack of the full moon. That's when you had the most water, but the practicality had long since settled into a superstition. The February moon was coming up, and all was made ready. Barrels of grease had been spread on the ways, and props were loosened. A platform was at the bow, where Mrs. Soule would stand with an armful of roses and smash the bottle of champagne. On the launching day every last person who came into the yard looked first to see if the champagne was there, because Maine was strictly dry and it was hard to get. It was — braided inside long silken ribbons that reached into the forestays. There was a band, and some fifteen thousand people. That's more than came to see the *John A. Briggs* launched.

I had no business going aboard the *Sintram*, but nobody told me I mustn't, and I did. Nobody ordered me off, so I stayed. I stood in the ankle-deep wet slush of the night before and felt the day grow colder. The slush turned to ice as I stood in it. Then I heard a man shout, and suddenly the *Sintram* echoed with the pounding of hundreds of hammers at her shores. This was the first round — it would not start her moving. A man at every shore and a hammer to every man, but there would still be the main props to hold her in place. As suddenly as the noise began, it ceased; and then I could hear the voice of the Rev. Daniel Chisholm addressing God from the launching platform. There were no public address systems then, and ministers knew how to pray so you could hear them. God was reminded of the seafaring heritage of the town, complimented for His kind attention in the past, and asked to place His approval on this newest venture. The prayer was larded with salty maritime allusions about fair winds, calm seas, safe landfalls and quiet havens after storm. The instant the Amen fell the men under the *Sintram* went back to hammering, and now she was to be launched.

It took perhaps ten seconds, then the the hull under my cold feet began imperceptibly to move. There was no shiver, no shake — suddenly it seemed to me the people and the buildings and the trees were all sliding back away from me. I couldn't see it from the deck, but the timbers under the keel were smoking and the grease on the ways was melting — the tremendous friction had its effect. But above all else, there was absolute silence. Mrs. Soule had smashed the bottle and cried out, "I name thee *Sintram*; go, and sail far and home!" and then there wasn't a sound throughout the whole yard. The huge vessel, touching only the smoking grease, slid silently toward the sea, stern-first.

But the instant the stern touched the tide, everybody let loose. The band played, but the cheering thousands drowned it out. Fire engines cranked their sirens, but the shouting covered the wailing. The donkey engine in the sawmill let go with all it had, and you could see the steam in the air above the whistle but not hear the toot. I looked overside, and timbers from the cradle were popping up in the seething swirls under the *Sintram*. There is a moment in a launching when a ship is neither ashore nor afloat. Held still by the long sloping ways, her stern is beginning to be buoyed. Once her prow leaves the ways she will float as her builders meant, and her masts will be straight to the sky. The *Sintram* now had straight masts.

But then her snubline parted, and her momentum took her across the harbor and she bumbled ingloriously into the mud. I felt her slow as the keel hit. I could look back to the shipyard and see the firemen squirting water on the smoking ways, and I thought the gap in the yard was small for such a big ship. The platform looked odd, standing there against nothing at all, and the people all gone from it. I could see the people — they were all going on toward the yacht club, because that's where the food was.

There was no feast aboard the *Sintram*. A couple of workmen were stuck there with me — they had meant to help warp her back to the dock with the line — and there was a *Press-Herald* photographer who had forgotten to bring any film. We froze, and we starved. As the tide ebbed the *Sintram* leaned a little, but not much. We called, and a few gay voices called back cheerily. Bingle Bubier came in from fishing later and we hailed him. He came alongside and we slid down a hawser into his boat and he ran us ashore. At the yacht club they told us the food was gone and the party was over.

When they yanked the *Sintram* off the mud they finished rigging her, and she stood out one morning and was a beautiful, beautiful thing. Humpy Dixon, our harbormaster, went up attic and brought down the old saluting gun, and he touched it off when the

Sintram passed Pound o' Tea and Punkin Nub. It had been so long he didn't know if it would shoot or not. The *Sintram* went to Norfolk and they loaded her with coal, and on the way back she foundered off Jersey. That was the end of that. The insurance company was generous and our businessmen got most of their money back. But I guess that's not the point. The point is that I was launched aboard a five-masted, State-o'-Maine schooner — and such a short time ago I'm here to tell about it. And I believe, absolutely, that some day when the World and the Universe and the Contiguous Regions are probated, the last thing God does before He lowers the boom will be to have some Maine shipbuilders turn Him out just one more sailing vessel.

THE PIPE ORGAN

THE most moving religious experience of my boyhood came when I was converted from a Congregational first baseman to a Baptist left fielder. The new coach carefully distinguished the things that were Caesar's and the things that were not, and he stood us in a circle before the game and asked divine blessing on our efforts and spiritual guidance in what we were about. We lost the game, seven to nothing, to the Universalists, who had not prayed. I decided that God aligns Himself with the team that has the best pitcher.

The Sunday School League taught us small baseball, because the coaches were always civic-minded church leaders who wanted to work with the boys, but since we couldn't play unless we attended the sabbath instruction hour we did get to know something about the Bible. My hereditary persuasion was Congregational but I was playing on the bench most of the time, and there was an opening with the Baptists.

I was a Baptist only one summer, and hit .276. Otherwise my spiritual guidance was in the lackluster traditions of the early parish meetings, but I made out. When I was twelve I was handed the grave responsibility of pumping the pipe organ, which I did for several years.

Recently the Arthur D. Little Company, an authority above reproach, published a report telling what every pipe organ pumper knows — that an electric organ is not an organ. It is a cunningly contrived device, but it is not an organ. The pipe organ derives its quality not only from the balanced air in its tubes, but from the resonance of its own being, its stature and its surroundings. The delayed action of its valves, nothing like the clipped constancy of electrical switches, is itself a musical asset. Adding an electric motor and a blower to an old pipe organ will not materially detract from its quality, but it does bump the small boy who once jerked the handle up and down to provide the wind. Without me, there would have been no music. When the minister arose and said, "Let us sing hymn number one-oh-two," he was paying supreme tribute to my reliability. Had I failed, religion would have halted.

My Congregational church had a lovely organ, and still has it. More sensitive communicants have several times rebuked efforts to replace it with an electrical substitute. It does have a motor today, but what the motor does, I did. I lifted and lowered the wooden bar, smooth as a smelt, to thrust wind into the mammoth bellows. The bellows was loaded with rocks from a stone wall to force the air into the pipes when Miss Pratt depressed the keys. For the light background music, obbligato to the prayer, this was no great demand, but when she bore down on the Doxology my tongue would be hanging down like a red necktie and I would get a stitch in my side. Sometimes she would pull out the Grand Diapason when I wasn't expecting it, and before I could get the rocks back up in sight again things would be nip and tuck.

But other boys had to sit with their parents in the pews and squirm through the admonitions while I was out of sight behind the big pipes, around to the rear of the vestry. During the non-musical parts of the services I was free to wander about and give the sermon the disinterest it deserved. I could look out the back window and see the discarded Christmas tree and the ash barrels. Or I could apply myself to the Sunday School Library.

I hope somebody, somewhere, has saved an old Sunday School Library intact. Ours was foolishly disposed of one time by a liberal minister I shall always hate, whoever he was. I suppose he thought the time had gone and the collection was useless. After all, we now had a town library. But this foolish man threw away one of the finest collections of topnotch instruction for the adolescent. My Sunday School Library was my introduction to sin, evil companions and the lust of the flesh. In order to get into a Sunday School Library a book had to be written by a minister, and it had to deplore wickedness and reward piety. This morality was conveyed by graphic enumerations of sin which, by rejection, brought the hero or heroine to grace, redemption and the sweet happiness of eternal bliss. Virtue won its reward, but the girl who went the farthest repented the most, and made the best example. I used to pump the organ up to the time of the sermon, and then I'd pick down a book and learn about sin.

One book in particular was a dandy. It was about a pretty girl who went with a circus. She escaped seduction about three times on every page as villain after villain tempted her, and between times she would fend off drunkards and gamblers, thieves and fiends, and assorted debauched persons who make up the typical circus company. Through all this she remained sweetly pure, and one day in a small Indiana town she married a minister who knelt and prayed with her in the tanbark, and she remained there to help him in the rewarding work of his poor parish. Sunday after Sunday I snatched nuggets from this treasury, and I used to hide the book behind some old crepe paper so nobody else could take it out until I finished it.

On Thursday evenings I had to pump for choir rehearsal, but there wasn't any time for reading then. There was more pumping for rehearsals than for the Sunday services. The choir was pretty bad. There was one man with a deep bass voice but he had no tone, and he couldn't carry a tune with a clam rocker. Whatever the tune was, he'd end each line on a low blat like a stuck foghorn. Miss Pratt had a way of chording something that eased the thing off, but it gave an odd twist to the traditional tunes. The choir was composed mostly of good, Christian intent, and voices were secondary. The twenty-five cents I got for pumping on Sunday included my services for the rehearsal.

But it also included pumping for the tuner when he came every summer. He was a small man and he would crawl inside the organ and talk to himself and wipe and clean, and he also talked to the organ. He'd put neat's-foot oil on the leather bellows, and rearrange the rocks. Finally he would set all the big front pipes back into place, patting each as it seated home, and then he would turn to me, bow deeply, and say, "And now, if you're ready, sir — at your service!" It was the only time I, the pumper, was ever acknowledged throughout my whole musical career at the handle. Miss Pratt acted as if she didn't know I existed. The minister never let on he knew that anybody pumped. On the steps, after meeting, people would say to him, "A fine message, Reverend — very fine indeed!" But nobody ever shook my hand and said, "You blew well today!" Only the organ tuner ever conceded. He as much as admitted that without me he could do nothing — when I was quite ready he would play.

Oh, what beautiful music we made! None of your church stuff now; but overtures from *William Tell's*, marches from *Aïda's*, lullabies from Brahmses, great whooping storms from Beethovens, and sweet melodies from Stephen Fosters, trailing off into the farthest big beams of the high roof. He would yell to me through the pipes and tell me what he was going to play next, and I would lay to and provide the wherewithal. The old church rocked on its foundations with the greatest music ever written — and not another soul in town knew what was going on. I would come in the next Sunday and pump for the sedate reverence of Isaac Watts, and wondered what the congregation would do if the old organ suddenly began showing what it could really do.

When the organ tuner's last sweet whimper died in the rafters he could call through the pipes to me, "The child is born!" I thought it was a religious remark, probably something to do with Christmas. So I would come around into the church and he would say, "I trust the question of emolument is adequately handled by the church treasurer?" I assured him I was being paid regularly, and the annual pipe organ inspection was over. In afteryears I went through the old parish records, and I was grief-stricken to learn that my years at the pump handle remain anonymous. Sunday after Sunday the entry runs the same: "Boy to pump — 25¢." I wish they had set my name down. It was my first steady job, or position. My mother always made me put the twenty-five cents in the Sunday School collection.

That old church ceased to be its own true self some years back. Arising from the pseudo-Calvinistic differences of the Reformation, the Congregational Church was protestant of Protestantism. It came to

America with the Pilgrims, but gained its true separatism when parishes were established in the backlands. Each congregation was its own boss, and if it wanted a choir that sang off-key it was nobody's business anyplace else. The working aspects were established in the "parish," which had self-perpetuating trustees who handled all the business. In the earliest days the parish meeting was also the town meeting, but the rise of Baptists and Universalists forced a division of church and town. But each Congregational church still operated out of its annual parish meeting, and anybody could be a member of the parish without being a member of the church. My father was such, and one year they made him parish treasurer and the fighting began almost immediately.

First off, our family found there was a fiscal aspect of devotions. After services that first Sunday my father didn't make for the front steps to shake hands with the minister — he scooted down front to count the collection. New shingles, paint jobs, coal bills and all other parochial activities were recurring obligations, and Father took his position seriously. He began going to Wednesday night meetings, dropping in after the testimonials to pick up the coins — as if he didn't trust the minister to handle the funds. And Father was a principal in the final gasp of the old parish-church relationship in our town. The minister arose in parish meeting one time to offer an opinion, and my father objected. "He's not a member of this parish," my father told the moderator. It was true, and Dad was right, but it was a lost cause. "He's just a hired man," said my father. The next year the nominating committee bypassed my father, found a new treasurer, and things began going to pot. The choir took to wearing robes, and the minister even affected a clerical gown. There began to be talk of centralizing the authority and amalgamating with other creeds. In time Mainers will let their precious town meetings go, just as they allowed their parishes to lapse, and for the same reasons.

My father's implication that ministers might be light-fingered with the collections was intended as a pleasantry, and I am sure he was probably more sincere about his obligations to the church than many another who talks more about it. He felt, with some logic, that a man who worked for light and heat and rent and $500 a year wasn't necessarily elevated into a business tycoon by spiritual fervor, and certainly not into an intellectual giant. The sermons of my youth lead me to agree with the latter. I used to sit there, until I got my pumping job, and think of better ways to say the same things. I used to wonder what God would think if somebody called Him You instead of Thou. But such critical thoughts were not the usual thing. Sunday Services were a time for the skinflints and the widow-baiters, the farmers and the factory people, the bankers and the halfwits, and each and all to sit for a time in spiritual democracy. The peace and quiet made them immune to bad singing and poor preaching. I returned to the church once in after-times, and the choir robes and the pulpit gown hadn't changed much. The minister shook my hand on the way out and said he was glad to see me, and that he hoped I would find opportunity to join the fellowship more often. I didn't tell him I used to pump his organ and read the library books.

THE ASCENSION

O NCE, and only once, I heard a rip-snorting sermon in our church. I also saw Jesus ascend
into Heaven there, and it was full as good a miracle
as the original performance. I do not mean to be
profane — all this was deeply significant, and important at the time. The ascent of Jesus is always
associated in my mind with the hot dog.

The reason we had poor preaching was, of course,
a simple one — our pulpit was a haven for broken-
down ministers who were going to retire after one
more year and had long since accepted the frustra-
tions of their lot. We never had anybody with the
fire and zeal of untried youth, and if we got anybody
at all young he was looking already for a better
chance. Our ministers used to preach about burning
bushes and chariots of fire, but they never got any
steam up. "That was a fine message," people would
say to them on the porch of the church, but it hadn't
been a fine message at all. I used to think it might be

fun to be a parson and have nothing to do but deliver a sermon I'd had all week to prepare, and I supposed I could get a little mustard into it. I knew there was no money in it, but I felt a man able to convert miserable sinners to the cause of righteousness ought to be able to persuade a finance committee to raise his pay.

About the time my thoughts were ranging like this the Fagoni family came to town. Nobody knew where they came from and at first we thought they were Gypsies. But they were Eye-talians. Until they arrived the only Italian we knew anything about was Valente the banana man, who lived two towns away and drove a white horse and wagon through once a week to peddle fruit. I knew Valente very well, and ours was the only house in town he had ever entered. He was a little fellow with a big moustache, probably younger than I thought he was, and we youngsters weren't so much taken with his brand of English as we were with the fact that his horse understood Italian. My father used to call him Garibaldi, and Valente would laugh and make-believe draw a sword. One day Valente drove into the yard in bitter cold weather and he looked as if he were frozen to the seat. He had a lighted lantern under the blankets that covered his oranges and bananas, but nothing to warm him. Father asked him to come in and get warm, and he did. Dad brought up a glass of cider from the cellar and mulled it with a red-hot poker from the stove and Valente drained it off and got a little tipsy. Always after that Mother would get fourteen oranges for a dozen and Valente would stand in the door and visit as if he were hoping for some more cider. He told us about the little village he left in Italy and how he afterwards sent back for his wife, and how the children were doing in school here. He would say, "Pretty good-a for a wop!" Father told us it was all right for Valente to call himself a wop and a dago, but that we must never do it. "The old fellow could buy and sell half the town," he'd say, "and he did it all in twenty years selling bananas." One time Valente brought some pomegranates and showed us how to eat them. We didn't like them much, until we found out he brought them just for us — they weren't for sale. Valente introduced grapefruit to our town. The first load he brought didn't sell, because nobody knew what they were, so he gave them away with instructions how to eat them. The next time around they sold. So we thought Valente was quite a man, and we respected him probably more than anybody else in town did, and that was all we knew about Italians.

The Fagoni family was something else again. Papa Fagoni always wore striped gray pants with sharp creases, pointed buttoned shoes, a fancy vest, and a flower in his lapel. His hat was black, and rakish. He was short and roly-poly. If he looked like a dressed-up melon, Mama Fagoni looked like a Hubbard squash. She was forever laughing, if anything was funny or not. And the children were like a flock of young partridges — scurrying, scampering, chattering; gay and lively. Like young partridges, you couldn't get one off by himself. We tried to take some of the boys on a cookout, but they always wanted to come home right away. I never tried to get one of the girls off alone, because truth to tell I was afraid of them. A couple were about my age and they were mighty pretty — so pretty we wondered how Papa and Mama Fagoni did it — but they had a way of smiling and looking very wise about the eyes, and it made us back off. And they talked Italian amongst themselves so we always surmised they were discussing us. They moved into town with gusto, spoke to everybody cheerily from the first day, and accepted us all as longtime friends and neighbors. Soon Papa Fagoni built a small shop on Main Street. He suspended a bunch of bananas in one window, filled up a tobacco and cigar counter, and had a steam peanut roaster that whistled out on the sidewalk. In the other window he had a hot-dog cabinet, and his hot dogs were delicious. They were the first hot dogs anybody ever sold in our town, as distinguished from frankfurters by the pound in the meat markets. The whole family worked in the store, and you never knew if Mama Fagoni would fit your weenie in the roll or if it would be little Joe, who had to stand on a chair to do it.

The town was amazed when the Fagoni family turned out the first Sunday and attended services at the Congregational church. We thought all Italians were papists, and with all the children the Fagoni family had, they had to be. But they came marching in, two by two, with Papa and Mama Fagoni bringing up a proud and ample rear, and Luther Pennell, our usher, led them to a middle pew — the longest we had. They filled it all the way across — a happy, bright-eyed family of outlanders who seemed a trifle too joyous for our sedate old house of worship. They were the first people I ever saw in church who didn't look as if their feet hurt. And when it came time for the hymn, didn't they sing! Papa Fagoni was better than Caruso, and the shingles jingled when he took a high note. Mama Fagoni was alto, true and rich, and she hit every note dead center. There was more music in that one pew on one hymn than our autonomously competent choir had produced in a hundred years. Everybody stopped singing to listen, and the Fagoni family sang on alone. They belted it out with the inspired fury of a Milan premiere, and God on his throne must have leaned down that morning to find out what in the world was going on in our church. It was beautiful.

It turned out that Papa Fagoni was himself a minister. Just how his latinity arrived in the Congregational pulpit was never cleared up, but he had a D.D. degree and was the real thing. He'd quote Scripture when we bought bananas and hot dogs. One day little Tony volunteered, "There are no swearwords in *our* language!" I never doubted it. The Fagoni family lived a strong Christian life amongst us, and set many a good example.

Then one day the Rev. William Brigham Faversham took ill, and word went around that there would be no sermon on Sunday. Papa Fagoni immediately stepped into the breach, and word went around again that there would be. A poster went up in the post office, and all Saturday afternoon the Fagoni children rang doorbells and told people Papa was going to preach. It worked, and we had the biggest turnout in history. Luther Pennell trotted his feet off finding seats, and had to open the rolling doors into the vestry for the overflow. He had to get Ed Davis to help him seat people. Minus Papa, the Fagoni family paraded in triumphantly, with the eldest boy, Luigi, escorting Mama, who beamed. And when Papa Fagoni came forth from the pastor's study to the pulpit he was dressed just as he dressed to sell bananas and cigars — even to the flower in his lapel. Such haberdashery and such ostentation was unique in the long tradition of our sedate rostrum.

The text that morning was from Chronicles. Other pastors had belabored the Chronicles before, but always with the seeming approach that one thing is probably no worse than another. Papa Fagoni handled himself as if this were going to be the definitive sample of the Christian pulpit at its best. For my money it was. He told how the Glory of the Lord filled the Temple of Solomon until the priests could not administer. A cloud of spiritual presence descended until a hundred and twenty trumpets fell into confusion and could not be heard. All the beauty and glory and magnificence of the newly finished temple faded to nothingness before the Glory of the Lord. Papa Fagoni let his tenor voice tremble as he described the silver and gold and the precious treasures, the cymbals and psalteries and harps, the doors and basins and lamps, the flowers and the sanctified white robes of the priests. But all was meaningless before the Glory of the Lord. Running back and forth behind the pulpit, which was too tall for him, he erected the whole House of God before our eyes, stone by stone and word by word, and the project had the bright sheen of Renaissance approval — love of beauty and form, joy in beholding precious things; the beating of gold, the soft touch of color on fresco, the melody of measured words sung to the lute and the lyre, the swish of brilliant silks along marble corridors, and the savor of spices and herbs in the sacred sanctuaries. It was fuller than a Medici dream. Yet all — all this — was lost in the Glory of the Lord which descended upon the holy place. Papa Fagoni was waving his arms over his head. The Glory of the Lord was in our church that morning, and I saw the wondering faces of stern old Calvinists turn and look at it. It shone best of all in the faces of the Fagoni family, who beamed all the while on Papa with a love and admiration that stood out about four feet on the average. And Papa Fagoni did the wisest thing a minister can do — he stopped before he was expected to. He spread his hands in a gesture of futility and said the Glory of the Lord was upon us, too, in our temple, and the beauty and the wonder of it quite silenced his tongue. "Let us make a joyful noise unto God," he said, and we turned to the hymn.

Our church never paid Papa Fagoni anything —

his was volunteer service. He filled in several times, and he would often take the vesper services in the vestry. As Easter approached he promised to show us his stereopticon slides of the crucifixion and the ascension. Stereopticons were still pretty good entertainment, and we didn't get to see them too often. We looked forward to the Easter show, and Papa Fagoni certainly didn't let us down.

He didn't tell the story that went along with the slides just the way we'd heard it so many times before. When he showed us the Mount of Olives he explained how olives are grown — how gathered and pressed, and about the several kinds of olive oil. He then gave us a little recipe for salad dressing. It was a new twist for Easter.

Then he came to the last slide in his lecture, and it showed Jesus after the resurrection, standing among the disciples on the mountain. Jesus in this slide looked wondrously like a Léopold Flameng gentleman out of the *Decameron,* and the disciples suggested Michelangelo, da Vinci, Cellini, Galileo, and so on. "Then Jesus blessed them," said Papa Fagoni, "and then . . ."

Then he reached behind his projector and fumbled at a little handle attached to the slide, and before our very eyes Jesus was jerked sky-high behind a cloud. I saw it, and I believe. In the spell Papa Fagoni wrought that evening in the vestry it was just as real as real can be. It was the only time I ever heard applause during a worship service.

Have you ever seen a flock of young partridges in

the woods? They scamper about and run together again, and they are everywhere at once. But you turn your eyes away and they are gone when you look back. The Fagoni family, one morning, was gone. Nobody knew where. They had packed up, peanut roaster and all, and disappeared.

THE BIG HIT

THE real reason we liked the Sunday School League was the equipment. We could play scrub baseball any time, involving about the same boys, but we didn't get to use the catcher's mask and the bats. The deacons in charge of the youth programs were careful to collect all equipment after the games. And they had small, but adequate, funds to replace lost balls. If we were playing scrub and knocked the hide off a ball we'd have to go down to Dave Longway's garage and beg friction tape to wind it, but in the Sunday School League there was always a spare ball. School equipment, of course, wasn't available during summer vacation, and we weren't old enough then to play with the town team.

Some of the church teams played sharp baseball, but some of the splinter groups had trouble mustering a team and they'd have to borrow a few players. The Word of the Spirit Church held Saturday as holy, and they wouldn't schedule a game for that day unless we lent them Jimmy Babcock to pitch. Jimmy was our best pitcher. He would mow us down three to an inning and grin at us, but we got to play. We had a teacher along then who sort of coached us, and he promoted this sporting attitude, and I'm glad. Athletics was not a cultural adjunct then, and taxpayers thought chopping wood and pitching hay were just as good and cheaper, so we didn't get too much sound coaching. This teacher told us, for instance, never to argue with an umpire, because it took time away from the fun of playing. I remember one game — I made a sensational running catch in left field, and doubled a man off second with a knothole throw. The enemy took exception, and after a rhubarb they walked off the field and wouldn't finish the game. This teacher said, "See? Now nobody gets to play, and the afternoon is wasted." It was even so. We won the game by a two-to-nothing forfeit score, but that's a poor kind of victory.

I could hit, but I didn't have any power. Put a man on third and I could usually bingle him home with a short one over second. This was the kind of hit I got off Jack Coombs, and if you want to look in the record books you'll find a lot of big-league players never did that well. Jack was a local boy and began playing baseball around town just the way I did. He and Levi Patterson looked good in high school, and at that time Colby College was looking for baseball talent. Jack and Levi went to Colby. They were both pitchers, and Jack once struck out twenty-four men in a nine-inning game. One time

Levi was telling about this and I said, "You were about as good, weren't you?"

"Oh, my, no," said Levi. "Most I ever struck out was twenty-two."

Jack Coombs went on to his fame with Philadelphia, while Levi returned to town and settled in as a businessman and State Representative. He was on the school board, and for a time was tax collector. And after Coombs retired he used to coach a semi-pro ball team here in Maine summertimes, and would stop around now and then to visit with Levi. And once a year we'd have the big hero back on our diamond for the Old Timers' game. The old timers would play the high school. It was a formidable team they turned out, not only in numbers but because Jack and Levi would show up in their old Colby uniforms and they were two of the best pitchers Maine ever saw. Our high school squad would be lucky to have fifteen boys, but the old-timers would come in flocks and squadrons, walking across the field with their favorite bats and gloves from yesteryear, and overpowering us by platoons and legions. Everybody in town was an old-time ballplayer.

This particular year Jack Coombs came on to pitch in the fourth inning. He was old and he was retired, but he was Jack Coombs and he was throwing with everything he had. He struck out Charlie Hawes with three pitches and everybody cheered. Bob Randall was catching Coombs, and he walked to the mound to hand the hero the ball and he said, "That's the old Jack-boy, that's the old stuff!" I stepped to the plate and dumped his first pitch over second, and was on base. I didn't hear Bob Randall say anything at that. But it's in the record book, and you have to do a little hunting to find somebody else today who bingled a hit off Jack Coombs.

Also in the record book is baseball's most unusual play. As left fielder, I made a put-out at the plate. It was easier than it sounds, and at the time was completely logical. We had a pitcher that year who was a find. He didn't have a thing on the ball except a rifle bullet, and most of us were too slight to catch him. He'd knock us right over. Tubby Bleaker was no ballplayer, but he had some heft, so we made him catcher and he didn't do too bad. If Tubby dropped a third strike he'd have to run halfway to first before he could throw that far, and a batter would beat him out. The wonderful thing about Clarence our pitcher was that he was cross-eyed and couldn't see very well.

So the coach got a can of yellow paint and painted the catcher's mitt. This was so Clarence could look in and see where he was supposed to throw. Tubby would hold up the yellow mitt and Clarence would squint to find it, and then he would drill the ball right into it. And since he was cross-eyed he did all this while appearing to gaze off into left field. About all a batter could do was wait to hear the ball hit Tubby's mitt and then swing. Tubby would recoil about two feet and then throw the ball to the third baseman, who would walk over and hand it back to Clarence.

So on this day somebody accidentally connected with one of Clarence's pitches and the ball shot back and caught Clarence full in the belly. It knocked the wind out of him and he stood there and hoo-hoo-hoo'd trying to get it back. The batter took first with no trouble, and seeing that confusion reigned he decided to go for two. The ball was on the ground at Clarence's feet, but he couldn't see it and didn't care anyway, so the first baseman ran in and picked it up. Then with great presence of mind the first baseman threw the ball to first base. Since there was nobody there the right fielder had to come in and chase it down, and by this time the runner was on his way to third.

We had a rundown between second and third for a time, but we threw the ball away and the runner started for home. Then we had a rundown between third and home, and by this time I had come in from left field and was backing up the catcher at the plate. Somebody threw the ball to me and I tagged the runner out when he slid in.

The spectators rolled around on the ground in hysterics, and Clarence kept asking, "What happened, what happened?" Guy Bean said he never saw anything on a baseball diamond so funny, and if I'd stop in at the store he'd like to do something to show his appreciation. I stopped in, and he gave me a long-fingered outfielder's glove, which I still have. I use it in Old Timers' games.

THE HEN SHOW

MAINE was ever a great place for pussy cats and biddy hens, and the reasons are about the same. The old mariners would see a new and interesting pussy cat in some far corner of the world, and they'd fetch it home. And aboard ship a little coop of laying hens was a good idea. But after cats and poultry landed in Maine their futures diverged. The peculiar genes of a cat thrust to the fore regularly, regardless of mongrel interludes. The beautiful white Persian asleep today on the fish-house roof may have every cat blood in existence in her mean and nasty veins, but she appears to be a true Persian. Maine people who would gladly give away three of her kittens are grateful when a tourist pauses and offers fifty dollars for one of them.

But hens are different, and the beautiful birds from strange lands are mostly gone from the Maine scene today. The hybridization of modern poultry took place in my time, and the love of fine feathers passed from the farmer's heart. It was a planned and contrived thing, and sad. I had a pen of ring-necked pheasants as a boy, and exhibited them in the poultry shows. They had been domesticated in the Orient centuries ago, and no doubt some ship's cook fetched a pair back to Maine. So also with Minorcas, Andalusians, Brahmas. As for the pheasants, the often-less-than-bright Maine Legislature one year made them a game bird. There had never been a wild pheasant in Maine. But when the forward-surging biologists of the new put-and-take school of game management got things coming their way they began "breeding" pheasants. They got a game farm, set up incubators, built fences, wrote scientific articles, and all at once the ring-necked pheasant was the property of the state. It was now illegal for a small boy to have a pen of pheasants. We had a game commissioner in those days who managed to get himself established as an "authority" on the rearing of pheasants, and he got written up in the sporting magazines for something we boys, and the Chinese, had been doing for years. Today the sport of pheasant slaughtering is well established in Maine and you can run your window up almost any morning and shoot one out of the lilac bush. With centuries of domestication behind them the beautiful things don't seem to realize they have been enacted back into a pristine position. They still think they are hens. The pheasant is delicious at table, but when we used to pick one of my home-grown birds and make a pie we didn't have the sporty flavor of birdshot.

We ate our hens, whatever kind. We picked the feathers off and stewed them with dumplings, and they had a richer flavor and heartier gusto than the fancy paragons of the new poultry industry. Fancy! Fancy was a word we used for pretty feathers and trueness to type. We put fancy birds in hen shows and competed for prizes and ribbons, and thousands of people came to see. I can remember barnyards with settees along the fence so people could sit quietly and watch the handsome hens and roosters, as spectators at an exhibition. I can also remember precisely when "utility" became a new word in the hen business. We used to tweezer the feathers off the legs of hens that weren't supposed to have feathers on their legs, and we'd wash White Orpingtons in laundry bluing — then we'd win prizes whether they laid or not, whatever their conversion factor might be. But suddenly the government experts and the cow-college professors began putting meat and production ahead of looks, and fine feathers no longer made fine birds. All agricultural exhibitions received stipends from the state, so these fellows had a threat, and one by one the poultry shows began "protecting their stipend" by offering prizes for utility as well as fancy. This was, of course, the end of the hen show. Now a bird could cop a ribbon, feathers on her legs or not, if she had wit enough to hump up and lay an egg while the judge was looking. A magnificent hen, true to her ancestral contours, could stand there in beauty and splendor, but a scrub hen in the next cage could lay an egg and beat her. Soon the poultry industry boomed into its present commercial prominence and the hybrid egg-machine sent fancy poultry into oblivion. You can look and look, but you can't find an American Dominique. They fed their rugged qualities into the bloodlines of all the new strains, and then went their way.

And you can probably look and look today and not find a boy of around fourteen years who knows how to hypnotize a hen. People herding hens these days don't have time for such idle amusement. But when Dick Marston and I were about that age we hypnotized a whole hen show, and it was well worth the doing. All you do is grab a hen between the palms of your hands, with her head away from you, and wave her gently in a circle. This calms her, and then you put her down on her side so her beak is extended along the floor, or ground. Draw an imaginary line with your forefinger away from the end of her beak toward infinity, and then gently lift your hands away. She will lie there motionless for quite some time, staring at the line and clearly hypnotized. It doesn't harm her, and when she snaps out of it she'll go to eating as if she just arose from a pleasant rest.

So about five minutes to two the afternoon the hen show opened, Dick and I started with the Andalusians and we went up and down the rows of wire pens as fast as we could until we came to the Wyandottes, and we hypnotized every bird in the show except the geese and ducks. It doesn't seem to work on them. At two o'clock the doors were thrown open to admit the waiting crowd, and consternation reigned. The officials came running, and Dick and I naturally joined in the great concern over what had happened. Probably an epidemic, they said. But then the birds began to rouse up, starting with the Andalusians, and the show went on.

Along about that time the 4-H Club movement reached us. The four H's stand for Health, Heart, Hand and Head, but our crowd went for Hens. They had a whole bookful of projects we might embrace — pigs, calves, corn, landscaping — and the county agent tried to get some of us to diversify, but we all had pet hens and we all settled on poultry management. We were a hen town in a hen state, surrounded by direct descendants of the original cocks and floozies brought home under sail, and we weren't about to be weaned.

Father let me have a two-pen henhouse on the knoll where my 4-H hens would be by themselves, and I had me twenty-five rose-comb Rhode Island Reds, plus two roosters of stature that would adorn

66

the Supreme Court. The high spot of my project was the day I got twenty-seven eggs from my twenty-five hens. Mother said I must have neglected to pick up the day before, but the day before I had collected twenty-five eggs. And the next day I got twenty-seven again. Everybody was counting my eggs and nobody believed me. Even the county agent said *hmm-mm-mm*. Years later when they invented "battery henhouses" and every layer had her own cage they found the old one-a-day notion was wrong. Good care can do better. Three and four eggs a day have been clocked. But the hens don't last long, and age rapidly.

This two-pen henhouse gave me the idea of the self-winding trapnest, which is my only major invention. To prove laying quality, producers of hatching eggs used to trapnest their birds. When the hen went into a nest she couldn't get out until the farmer let her, and at that time he could check her production. Some hens go into a nest on a *fausse-couche,* and these complicate the thing because they tie up a trapnest for others that would lay. And the farmer had to hang around all the time to keep letting hens out and making his checkmarks on the laying record. I gave the thing a lot of thought and went to work.

My self-winding trapnest was built into the wall between the two pens, and in the morning all the hens were in the near pen. A hen couldn't lock herself in unless she laid an egg, so the fakers created no problem. Once she laid an egg it dropped onto a thick plush I got from an old automobile seat, and the weight of the egg on a lever locked the entrance and opened the exit. No hen could pass into the second pen unless she laid an egg, and when she pushed through the wire exit she set the nest for the next one. All I had to do was check my hens back into the first pen every evening. I asked around how anybody got anything patented, and I saw myself ranging into the higher realms of riches, famous and dedicated to philanthropies. There's no getting around it, mine was a fine invention.

But about that time the whole philosophy of trap-nesting exploded, and all at once nobody was using trapnests any longer. I was the candlemarker looking upon the first incandescent lamp.

The next thing in my poultry career was the free trip to the 4–H Camp at the Eastern States Exposition in West Springfield, Massachusetts. They had a part of the fairgrounds set aside for Camp Vail, where state champion 4–H boys and girls were rewarded. When Dick Marston and I learned about this we decided to go, and all we had to do was become state champions. We decided to do a demonstration about culling poultry. The theme was simple — you didn't need a trapnest to tell if your hen was laying, you could examine her biologically. Our stage properties were two hens — a good one and a no-good one. And it's pretty hard to think up something to better that. We could make them squawk if the program needed pepping up, and then we could show people how to calm them down.

After some opening remarks in which we introduced each other wittily, Dick would bring up a hen and show that she wasn't living up to her duties. Her yellow legs and skin showed she was not drawing pigment to color egg yolks. Her moist, beady eye indicated no constant strain. Her feathers were smooth and straight, proving she spent too much time primping. Then the high spot of his oration came when he reversed the hen and displayed her vent. Vent is a good 4–H Club word, and is a euphemism if I ever heard one. Dick would stand there as if he had a feathered Kodak and was posing a group picture. Sometime if you want to learn what stagecraft is, part the feathers on a hen's backside and expose her to a roomful of people. It is electrifying. To me and Dick it was amazing to watch a crowd inspecting a hen's anus for the first time and acting as if they did it every day. At this point Dick would go into a sly welter of double-talk and discuss the latus rectum with great delicacy, and point out that frequent ovulation entails wear and tear, and this hen was obviously inactive in this department.

In my turn, I fondled a "good" hen. Her skin was pale and bleached, for yolk after yolk had drained her substance. Her eye was parched and dull, showing the effect of constant strain. She had no time to primp, so her feathers were unkempt and bedraggled. Then I would turn her around and the audience would gasp. She looked like the Hoosac Tunnel. This hen, they could readily see, was a dandy. Any farmer would be proud. I had an egg palmed and I would now produce it and hold it up for all to see, meantime turning the hen back into a more dignified posture. We invited a question period, passed out some government pamphlets urging higher egg consumption, and closed the show. We won the county championship, went on to win the state championship, and had our trip to West Springfield. Fortunately two pleasant girls from the town of Brooks won the distaff competition that year and went with us, but unfortunately the trip was closely chaperoned by government extension specialists.

It was not rising competition, or disgust at the trends, which put me out of the hen business. It was an owl. One morning in the spring of the year I found a dozen or so of my beautiful hens dead in a corner of the yard, their heads pulled off and their crops opened. That would be an owl. It is illegal in Maine to set pole traps without a permit from the state, but I didn't wait to write to the capitol. I got me a spruce pole about fifteen feet long and I put it up right by the dead hens, and I set a steel skunk trap on the top of it with the chain securely stapled. Hawks and owls scanning a poultry yard will first perch and the top of a handy pole suits them fine. The next morning I had my owl — a great brute two feet tall, and the jaws of the trap closed on his talons. He was hanging head down when I found him, and he snapped his beak and screwed his neck around. Then he tried to fly away. But the length of chain caught him up short and he flopped down again to snap his beak some more.

Dr. Gilchrist used to tell about a patient he had

one time with a carbuncle on his neck. The doctor got ready to lance it and said, "Now take a deep breath and grit your teeth, because this is going to hurt." Then he lanced it. But the patient never moved a hair, and Dr. Gilchrist said, "I guess you don't know what pain is!"

"Oh yes," he said. "I know what pain is all right."

"For instance?" said Dr. Gilchrist.

"Well, one time I scooched down in the woods to answer a call of nature, and I was right over a bear trap, and it closed on me. That really hurt. In fact, I think that was the second most painful experience of my life."

"Should think it would be," said Dr. Gilchrist. "And what do you think was the first most painful experience of your life?"

"That was when I come to the end of the chain."

My owl had come to the end of his chain. I laid the twelve-gauge to my cheek and blew most of his feathers off, and thus repaid him for murdering my hens. I was all through being a poultryman. The era was done; the hen shows were folding up. We could buy a plucked chicken and didn't need to pick a hen. By the time state inspectors began coming around in big automobiles to eradicate pullorum and salmonella my two-pen henhouse had fallen in, trap-nests and all. But you can still find true-to-type pussy cats along the coast of Maine.

THE GRAVEL PIT

ONE happy February morning news ran about that
Secretary Potter would be a candidate for road
commissioner. Spring had made a false start that day
and unseasonable mildness permitted Secretary to
throw open the big doors and air out the livery stable
a good two weeks ahead of usual. The good feeling
that came upon him as he filled his lungs with the
bright promise of vernal salubrity quite carried him
away. He felt public spirited. The town wouldn't
have given him six serious votes, and not above eight
as a joke, so the announcement wasn't much of a
threat.

But it was significant. Lem Bradley had been our
road commissioner for twenty years and the idea of
any competition, however frivolous, was distasteful
to him. Besides, maybe Potter knew something. Lem
approached Secretary at once and said, "I understand
that you propose to seek sustenance at the public
teat!"

Secretary Potter admitted his desire to hold office, and Lem said, "But why me?"

"Because," said Secretary, "you ain't going in again."

My father was always astute at forecasting public reactions, and when he heard about this he concluded Potter was probably right. Secretary was in an excellent spot to survey and assess things, and he must have detected growing resentment against Bradley. If the town had to find somebody else, it would throw the thing open, and even Potter might stand a chance in a wide-open contest.

We didn't have any such class in school then as "American Democracy" with textbooks approved by the administration. But every year just before town meeting time in March our teachers would run us through some mock sessions. We'd elect town officers amongst ourselves to find out how ballots are cast, and then we'd debate a few "articles" and raise money. This probably taught us nothing about politics, but it did give us a valuable grounding in parliamentary rules. Throughout Maine today one of the gravest threats to perpetuation of basic democracy is the lack of such knowledge amongst new voters. Boys and girls come out of school today full of wide theories about policy and issues, but they don't know a privileged motion from a constable's bond. I have even seen a teacher of civics rise in town meeting, make harangue, and sit down without offering a motion. This leaves the moderator high and dry, and causes the town clerk to weep. It was not so in our time, because in addition to the little workouts in school Town Meeting Day was a holiday and most of us went and watched. Today the loudest wail over high taxes comes from industrialists who keep their shops open and prevent their workers from going to vote against absurdities. I was eleven when I started selling tobacco in town meeting. Artie Mitchell ran the newspaper and tobacco store, and he fixed me up with a tray of smoking and eating tobacco and I hawked the stuff at a nice profit. I did this every town meeting until woman suffrage hit us, and after that nobody smoked. I took the tray back to Artie intact and he said, "Damn women!" He gave me a five-cent Tootsie Roll and said, "Here, just so you ain't skunked."

We didn't use the Australian ballot in our meetings. It cost more and took too long. But the law made us elect all officers by majority vote — which you don't have to do with the booths and a secret ballot. A plurality wasn't good enough. And the year Secretary Potter ran for road commissioner this majority rule turned out to be a problem. It took us all summer to elect a successor to Lem Bradley.

The road commissioner's job was a good one. He got a stated salary, but there was a chance to pick up a kickback here and there. He didn't have anything to do except look for places to dump gravel, and then see that it got dumped. Highway engineering, then, met its greatest challenge in nailing three planks together to make a culvert — as we said, culbert. But Lem had enjoyed the sinecure too long. Towns frequently like a change, for no reason. And Secretary Potter had sensed something brewing. My father said, "Wonder who we can get to run?"

Almost everybody ran. One by one names were nominated from the floor, including Lem Bradley's. When Whisperin' Gleason arose and nominated Secretary Potter with an impassioned address that drowned out a train going by the applause was tumultuous. A stranger to our town would have misjudged the ovation as election by acclamation. But in the vote, Secretary got a total of five. You can't always tell what a town is cheering for.

But there was no majority. Lem Bradley would continue to hold office until his successor was elected and qualified, so the meeting adjourned to the following Saturday to vote again. Saturday after Saturday they kept trying, but nobody came out with a majority. Then Secretary Potter announced that he would withdraw and "throw his support" to Maynard Matthews, who was getting eight votes. Then Maynard dropped out. Indeed, along in July Lem Bradley dropped out. He conceded. And when my father's candidate dropped out Dad went to A. W. T. G. Clarke, who was gaining every week, and said, "My man's out, I'll do what I can for you." A. W. T. G. Clarke was otherwise known as Alphabet Clarke, and he won a majority on the next cast. He took Bradley's place and worked the customary reforms — which means that he fired the old crew and hired a new one. In addition, the next week he came up and laid a new sidewalk in front of our house. I suppose such things are well studied in Problems of Democracy classes. At the time I thought it was a good thing to know about, and I often allow it to guide my thinking. Alphabet Clarke got reelected in March, and the next May I asked him for a summer job on the road work. He said he was swamped under by similar requests, but he could use me for a day or two on the Beech Hill construction. I reported to the gravel pit the day after school let out, and shoveled gravel in the town pit for two summers.

First, I had to buy a shovel. I went to Steve Mitchell's — he sold everything — and found I had an esthetic choice. He had some with green handles and some with red handles. "Most of the town crew uses the red," Steve told me, "but I never see it speeded 'em up any — why don't you be different and take a green?" The shovels came in a bundle of twelve, half red and half green, and Steve's pitch for individuality was because he had more green ones left than red. I took a red. There wasn't a scratch on the oil-smooth blade, and the handle had never felt human skin. The job began at seven A.M., and I was one of four who stood by the banking and hove gravel into blue tipcarts until noon. At one o'clock we began again and continued until five-thirty. This earned me fourteen dollars a week, or twelve-fifty if I took Saturday afternoons off. I never did. As soon as we loaded a cart another would back in, and the only hilarity came if we could throw on so much the horses couldn't budge it. Usually the teamsters would pull out, to avoid this, while we were still shoveling, but now and then one of them would stay just a mite too long. It was dull, methodical, rhythmical idiot-work, and until my muscles settled in I was ungodly lame. The first few nights I'd twitch in my little attic room from cramps, and shovel just as much as I did daytimes. Through the summer our only respite was rainy days, and now and then an afternoon thunder-shower. I carried my lunch in a pail and ate as much as a horse. And along in mid-August, Alphabet Clarke said, "Better get yourself another shovel, boy, you're dripping more'n you're heaving!" The pin gravel had worn the blade of my shovel out. This time I got a green one, because Steve Mitchell didn't have any red ones left.

The second summer I did this the truck came into the picture. Roy Marston, Dick's father, had a Model T truck with extra rear-end gears, and on a down-hill cant it would haul about a half-yard of gravel without boiling its hood off. Roy was far before his time, but he did a selling job on Alphabet Clarke, and got a chance to show what he could do on road-work. Roy admitted his load was smaller than a cart's, but he said he could make more trips, and at the end of the day he'd haul more than a team. The test wasn't really fair, and we all knew it. The teamsters saw their profession facing oblivion, so they chewed things over and devised strategy. First, they would trot a little. If you saw a team meander-ing along, horses in semi-slumber and the driver asleep on the seat, you knew they were working for the town. But with the truck threatening them, they cantered all day. They also contrived to freeze Roy out of his turn in the pit. Time after time he'd **have** to wait to get loaded. So at the end of that first day we shovelers were pooped so our eyeballs hung down, and all we had proved was that teams can outhaul a truck. We had, however, proved it conclusively, and the teamsters were overjoyed.

But Alphabet Clarke had eyes, and he asked Roy to come back the next day and try again. He shifted the roadwork off to the other end of town, about two miles — and that was too far to canter a horse all day. Dick drove his father's truck that day, looking about nine feet tall with pride and glory, and he began coming into the pit three and four times to the horses' once. During lunch hour they had to put new bands in the truck's friction clutch, and they added a quart of oil about every fifteen minutes all day. The engine was hotter than a skunk. Long before the day was out the teamsters were downcast. They were reaching for any argument, and the last one of all was that the truck stank. They would sniff at the gasoline fumes, the exhaust, the hot metal and the aroma of cooking petroleum oil, and act as if it was going to make them vomit. Then they would back in a sweaty team that promptly humped up and fouled the pit, and drive off to leave us the assessment of distinctions. Before that summer was out we were loading two trucks, and then three.

Years later the town bought a mechanical gravel loader, and I went and watched it work with much interest. It did put some people out of work, but it was a kind of work I can't say I truly relished. I'm glad I worked for the town in the gravel pit, because it was instructive and at the time profitable. When Alphabet Clarke gave me my last check (with one day out because it rained) he said, "I didn't think you'd last a week. I only took you on because your father was on my side." In September and October I would sit in school with my book open and pick at the rough, hard, ridged calluses on my hands and fingers. My skin was beginning to soften again, and the tissue was freeing itself. At the time I didn't realize that this was a political plum.

THE DOODY CAPER

Although the population of my town is now about what it was then, the annual budget for police protection has soared, and every few days they bring boys into court and charge them with horrible crimes. The truth is that in my time we didn't even have a policeman, and the total topic was covered by an annual appropriation of four hundred dollars for the night watch. This was Earl Buck, who wandered at moderate speed about the community with a clock on a leather strap over his shoulder and he "punched it in" with keys hung on chains here and there. This proved he covered his route, and at what time. His main function was to detect fires, and if he smelt smoke he would run to the hosehouse and ring the bell, and get the big doors open. The firemen would come running and then the place would burn down. The detection of crime and the apprehension of criminals was nothing Earl knew about or wanted any part of. Once some boys were plaguing him and he said,

"Now cut that out, or I'll have you arrested!"

Our state police was then in its infancy, and its only evidence was a goggled motorcyclist who stopped infrequently at Mary Collins's restaurant for apple pie and coffee and otherwise spent his time harassing out-of-state motorists, of whom there weren't many. Our only other constabulary was the deputy sheriff, who posed as a peace officer but whose real job was to keep voters congenial so they'd return the high sheriff to office every two years. The high sheriff of our county had the best political job in Maine, and he took re-election seriously. In each town he had a deputy to keep an ear to the ground. Indeed, candidates for other officers often rode the sheriff's coattails, so all hopefuls greased the sheriff's campaign palm liberally and he always had funds to spend, or lay by. No matter what lofty ideologies were being expounded by would-be governors and senators, the local issue boiled down to two men working their heads off for votes. One was the deputy sheriff and the other was the man who would become deputy sheriff if they could get the rascal out. In spirited contests, the sky was the limit.

The office of high sheriff would have been eliminated years ago in Maine if it didn't have this useful political value. It is a holdover from early England, and today the useful functions of the job could be done by a law clerk and a man to open windows in the courtroom. But instead of declining, the drain on the taxpayers flourishes, and deputies wear flashy uniforms, drive expensive automobiles with two-way radio, and play Dick Tracy around the clock. The state could save millions every year by outlawing sheriffs. In my time we were more honest about all this, and no deputy sheriff made any serious pretense of being a policeman. Arresting somebody might shut off a few votes.

Our deputy sheriff was a smooth handshaker who wore an overcoat with a plush collar and lived a life of impeccable decency with two maiden sisters who ran the W.C.T.U. He couldn't tell homicide from ribbon candy, but fortunately he never had to. I was personally and pleasantly, if innocently, involved in the only crime wave he was ever called upon to solve, and it amounted mostly to a long-winded interruption of my investigations into the ablative absolute. I was pondering this grammatical oddity at the kitchen table one evening when my sister came back from the front door and said Mr. Fellows was there and wanted to see me. Nobody in his right mind ever came to our front door, and my sister had to move a table and chair before she could open it. There he stood, his plush collar like a slightly lowered halo, and a stern, law-abiding frown upon him. "Good evening," he said to me. "I understand you play a good bit in the Maplelawn Cemetery."

Thankfully, I have no idea how a criminal investigation should really be launched, but I'm sure this wasn't it. Switching from Latin syntax to Maplelawn Cemetery in a fell swoop is not only an intellectual improbability, but it hampers a boy's general reactions. The last time I had been in Maplelawn

Cemetery was eleven months before, when I carried the flag for the Yarmouth Band in the Decoration Day exercises. I tried to think of all the wicked things I might have done which Mr. Fellows was approaching by this indirection. All I could think of was sending a naughty word on my spark coil, to fluster radio listeners, but I knew my coil was a secret only Charlie Hawes shared, and he wouldn't blab. Mr. Fellows eyed me during my deliberations as if he were gazing upon a convicted felon with the rope on his neck, and I could see he was picturing me as a ghoul who loved graveyards.

It turned out the tombstones in Maplelawn Cemetery had been violated. Somebody had pushed over a whole flock of them. News of this vandalism led many horrified citizens to insist that Mr. Fellows do something about it, and the quiet, calm existence of the deputy sheriff was rudely interrupted. The only thing he could think of was to go about and accuse every boy in town, and hope somebody would own up, but I have no idea why he started with me. My ablative absolute waited on the kitchen table for two hours while I was grilled on the front porch, and when Mr. Fellows decided I was too hardened a criminal to weaken under his tactics he went away. I put the table and chair back and went out to the kitchen and told my father about it. Dad got his back up and put his hat on and went right down to Mr. Fellows's house and told Mr. Fellows that if he didn't stop this nonsense he'd punch his nose so it would stick a foot out the back of his neck. Just the other day I saw a piece in the paper about a man who got ten years in jail for threatening a police officer, but Mr. Fellows took no action against my father. I guess he knew my father meant it. Anyway, I never had another visit from a deputy sheriff.

Mr. Fellows did putter around for a time, to placate the old ladies of both sexes who deplore the profaning of last resting places. We had Revolutionary War graves in our town all grown up to bushes and trees, and every year the town meeting would vote against spending fifty dollars to clean up the yard, but tipping over a gravestone was awful. But Mr. Fellows didn't ponder this oddity — he had the greater problem of deciding which course would jeopardize the fewer votes.

He got some help from a growing suspicion around town that the light snowfall of the past winter had let the frost penetrate deeper than usual, and that the stones had been hove by Mother Nature. Some of the monuments weighed a ton or more, so small boys weren't the most likely suspects. But he got more help from Doody Bailey. Doody stepped forward and said he would take all the blame. Yessir, yessir, he said, he done it. His confession was complete. He had taken a fifteen-year-old schoolgirl into the bushes back of the tomb, and to show her how strong he was he ran around in the moonlight and pushed over gravestones. Nosir, he would protect the name of this wayward child with his very life. Yessir, they could put him in irons and torture him, but his lips were sealed. That was all he'd say, and now that they had his confession the mystery was solved and the case was closed. Mr. Fellows wouldn't have to pry around no more. You can't convict a man on his own confession, Doody would say. Since Doody was eighty-eight years old the figment of the young girl was an amiable thought that many appreciated, and things turned out about as Doody expected. He was no friend of the W.C.T.U.

That Mr. Fellows happened to be the brother of the Fellows sisters with the W.C.T.U. context, was a firm political asset in Maine, where everybody has always voted dry and drunk wet. But it complicated his police function as it related to rum-runners. Our little seacoast town with its inlets was a favorite landing spot for the small boats that brought the booze ashore. The skippers carefully took all precautions. The high sheriff naturally had to make raids once in a while to prove his unflagging zeal for law and order, but it was not essential that he catch anybody, and if the skippers would just let him know where they planned to come in he would stage his raid at another place. Not only that, but he had to let the bootleggers know where he was staging the raid, so none of them would come ashore while he was around. If somebody fighting the temperance war chanced to see a strange man looking down a disused road, and called the sheriff to tip him off about a load, he would then naturally have to respond and sometimes he didn't get a chance to send out a decent alarm, but when that happened everybody understood and there were no hard feelings. It wasn't easy being a high sheriff in those times. So once in a while Mr. Fellows would have to leave his teetotal home and rush out to carry messages for his big boss.

Discretion and delicacy prevailed, but the bootleggers were also discreet. They were attuned to the nuances. Mr. Fellows would go into the drugstore and buy new batteries for his flashlight, and chance to remark in a loud voice that it was dark at night in the woods on Honker Point. Or he would pick up some new rubbers and say, "It's swampy down by Martin's Brook!" One time some bootleggers told Secretary Potter to have a team hitched to a wagon for them, and Mr. Fellows heard about it. He checked with the high sheriff, but they had no word of a landing. Mr. Fellows pumped Potter, but didn't learn anything, and as evening approached he played a hunch and went down to Grindle's Cove, which was a good place for hunches. Sure enough, he found a man hiding in the bushes, and Mr. Fellows upbraided him severely for conducting an illicit business without first checking in with the county authorities. The man seemed surprised to see Mr. Fellows, and at once introduced himself as a Federal alcohol and narcotics agent, and at this Mr. Fellows was equally surprised. Whatever was going on, the bootleggers never came that night for the team, although Secretary Potter kept them hitched in until after midnight. He always said a man came around two days later and gave him a box of cigars, so things must have turned out all right without the horses.

We had a court in our town, and at that time the

presiding justice was Judge Larrabee. He presided in rich Blackstone manner but he never had very much to do. He drew wills and deeds, took depositions as a notary, and did auctioneering. About the only criminals who appeared before him were tramps who purposely annoyed somebody so they could get three months in the reformatory, which would carry them through to warm weather again. Once in a while a railroad detective would roust a tramp off a freight train and demand punitive action. Judge Larrabee was always very hard on tramps. He would lecture the poor thing about mending his ways, sentence him to the reformatory, and then give the tramp money for a ticket on the next train. Most of them would buy the ticket, carry the committal papers, and show up for their term, but some would keep the money and ride to the reformatory on the brakebeams.

The judge's law office was also the courtroom, and when they were going to railroad a tramp we'd all crowd in to watch. Secretary Potter was the court crier. There was no provision for a crier in trial-justice courts, the lowest jurisdiction we had, but Secretary liked to do it. He would pound the desk with an Edgeworth tobacco can and yell, "Order in the court! Order in the court! All rise!" Judge Larrabee was always sitting right there at his desk because there was no retiring chamber except the toilet, and when we all stood up Judge Larrabee would stand up, too. Then he'd hold court.

As an auctioneer Judge Larrabee was without

equal. He'd hang on and get the last cent. He was witty, and knew how to keep the crowd in good humor. And when he walked out to start an auction everybody would stand up, just as in court.

We did have another kind of police officer — the state humane agent. Usually the governor and council at the statehouse would appoint somebody who loved cats, and there wasn't much activity in this department. Abuse of animals wasn't too common, but sometimes there might be neglect. And as with the deputy sheriff, there wasn't much to do unless somebody registered a complaint. Ruel Hanscom was our humane officer, and he told us boys his job was to keep people from milking a cow with more than two hands at a time. One time somebody came running to him with a complaint and said Asa Mumford was drunk and slit the ears of his horse with a knife. We all believed Asa was drunk all right, but the rest of the story seemed implausible. Ruel finished putting in a load of hay and went down to investigate. Sure enough, Asa had horses with sore ears, and Ruel promptly haled him before Judge Larrabee. The courtroom was jam-packed when Ruel told his story. It sure looked bad for Asa.

"Got anything to say?" asked Judge Larrabee, and Asa stepped up. It was the first time anybody had ever seen him dressed up. He even had a necktie on. Quite a handsome man. Nobody ever supposed he owned a suit, but he had one on. And under his arm he had a thick leatherbound book, with one finger stuck between pages. He opened the book on the desk before Judge Larrabee and pointed at a paragraph. "Right there," he said. Judge Larrabee looked at it, and then fumbled in his pocket for his other glasses and read it through carefully, his lips moving from word to word so a lip reader could easily have known what he was reading. Then he read it again, and he said, "Well, I'll be damned!"

Then he said, "Case dismissed!" The book Asa brought was an ancient compendium of home remedies for man and beast, and it said in severe cases of equine colitis, bleeding was advised, which could be induced by slitting the veins in the ears. The date on the book was 1715. Judge Larrabee was a judge for a long time, and this was by far his most momentous decision, and his most spectacular session.

Asa Mumford and his horses were in the news again later. He got hot one night and started for home in a blinding snowstorm, riding the bunk on his logging sleds. The sleds were empty, but Asa was loaded. The snow slanted in on a driving, bitter wind and Asa pulled himself into his mackinaw collar and let the horses slog along in knee-deep snow. They knew the way home. When they came to the railroad crossing the milk train snaked the horses right out of their harness and strewed them up the track for two miles. Asa sat there and never knew what happened and somebody found him half buried in snow yelling giddap. The railroad didn't know what happened until they found a horse collar and hames jammed behind a cylinder on the locomotive when the train reached Rigby Yards at Portland.

Some inspectors came around the next day, but it was too late to be of much help. Somehow I always thought this was harder on horses than slitting ears, but they didn't have Asa in court this time. And I would like to report that this experience prompted Asa to abstain, but I can't. The last time I saw him he was driving a buggy up the road at a good clip, singing a merry tune to his horse, and holding two lighted cigars in his mouth. Which, I suppose, shows you how we made out back before the police force became big business.

THE LOMBARD TANK

A NY normal boy growing up can number the teachers he loved on one hand. There will be some he almost loved. I also had some of the biggest dunderheads God ever allowed to be spawned — foisted on me and my classmates by the school board and superintendent without recourse. One of them was insane and went directly from our classroom to the wacky-house, but it took the school committee and the administration from September to February to find out what my class knew in two minutes. We tried to tell our parents, but they told us to stop making things up. I suppose education will improve as soon as parents stop listening to school boards and begin paying attention to their children.

Through the early grades we had some wonderful teachers. They helped us on and off with our mittens, inculcated the rudiments, and urged us gently along to higher things. We arrived in grammar school one otherwise lovely day to find a man teacher — a big, muscle-bound, muscle-brained boob who beat me up one day. He was as stupid as whale manure, but he had a certificate and therefore was a teacher. He left the room and threw the class on its own. I was wrapped up in a book, and as far as I knew the class was keeping the peace. My class was a bunch of wonderful children, and our record is serene and pure, and I'm sure nothing was going on that exceeded the required decorum. So I chanced to look up from my book and I saw this brainless gorm peeping in from the hallway through the half-open door, and I didn't suspicion anything so I smiled pleasantly at him, nodded, and turned back to my book. About that time he sailed into me, and if I hadn't been taught to relax he'd have killed me. When he got through I couldn't see for fifteen minutes. It's the only time in my life I ever saw a wild maniac in action, and the only answer I can give is that he was setting up a situation where he could demonstrate his authority. "There," he said. "That'll teach you to behave when I'm out of the room!" Nothing ever hurt me, body and soul, as he did. We were all afraid of him after that, and his effect as a teacher was nil. I used to sit and think how I would grow up, and some day I would find him, and I would kill him. I used to practice the happy smile I would smile as I did it.

Altogether too many of my teachers were on his side of the fence. Too many were unable to judge and assess young people. Too few knew how to fire us for learning and seeking. Too many insulted the bright days of youth with perfunctory, routine, color-less horse-dingle — were never equal to reaching and yearning with us. Day after day, hour after hour, we sat there asking them to be magnificent, and they seldom were. The few who were worthy are loved.

One day a horrified teacher found a sheet of paper pinned to the wall in the corridor, and on it was written:

> *It's naughty, but it's nice;*
> *You do it once, you do it twice —*
> *They do it in every nation*
> *To increase the population.*

Right away we knew something was afoot. We'd see two teachers with their heads together, and then two more. Tension was building, and we felt it. Then one by one pupils were tapped and fingered into the principal's office, and it came my turn. The principal handed me the sheet of paper and said, "When did you put that on the wall?"

I was scarcely old enough then to know what it was you did to increase the population, at least in foreign countries, but I know his question left me standing there with "that guilty look." "I never saw that until now, sir," I said.

"It's in your handwriting," he said.

It wasn't in my handwriting at all, and whoever had written it had taken pains that it wouldn't be in anybody's handwriting. "I never saw it before," I said, looking exactly as if I had never lied so beautifully.

He said, "Go to your seat."

I went to my seat and observed that all who came back from the inquisition looked just as guilty as I did.

Before this mystery ran its course another great mystery came hard upon. The science teacher used to put a clean sheet of paper on every desk at recess time, and the next class would have a one-question quiz. She would say, "Now, those who can spell laboratory may go there." Then we would write the word laboratory on the sheet of paper, and if we spelled it right we would pass out to the laboratory. Each day she had a similar gimmick, and I suppose it was good for us. But one day we came in after recess, and every sheet of paper had been scribbled on with a black wax crayon. Every day, day after day, the paper was defiled. On top of the sexy poem pinned up in the corridor this was altogether too much, and the inquisition was redoubled. Everybody had a guilty look. Then as I was sitting at my desk I had a real Sherlock Holmes deduction. This science teacher spent recesses lurking about to see who was fouling the sheets of paper, and if the paper still got fouled there could be but one answer. It had to be that teacher herself! I think the principal tumbled to this himself about the same time I did, because all at once the inquisition was over and we heard no more about the poem and the paper. I'm sure the poor thing, craving something she wasn't getting, despoiled the sheets of paper, but whether or not she put up the poem I never knew. I hope, if she did, that it brought her pleasure, for she needed it. I am indebted to her for one thing, at least — I have ever since been reluctant to leap to conclusions about the guilt of people who look guilty. The school board allowed her to finish out the year, and they gave her a wonderful letter of recommendation so she could get a job in another town.

The crazy teacher we had was Mrs. Chesney. Afterwards we found out the "Mrs." was gratuitous — she had never married. She was so homely only a blind man would marry her, let alone love her, and even he would have recoiled at the stench. She used perfume. Every time she walked by her desk she would pick up a bottle and dab behind her ears.

Although we had arrived at the portals of algebra, were reading the New England poets, and some of the girls had stopped going swimming with the boys, Mrs. Chesney kept us in kindergarten. A high spot in her academic program was the dramatization of "The Pied Piper of Hamelin." Mrs. Chesney said Browning was a fine poet — and I agreed because I was halfway through "The Ring and the Book" and

Miss Aldrich, our town librarian, was trying to find me something that would explain his "obscureness." I had started to memorize "The Bishop Orders His Tomb" so I'd have it ready for a speaking contest. So now we dramatized "The Pied Piper." Some of us were burghers and some of us were rats. It took weeks to get the thing right where Mrs. Chesney wanted it, but we were patient with her. I played the part of a man with a long pole who plugged up ratholes — I had the stick used to open and close the upper windows, and my part in every performance was to pull down the windows and air the room out from Mrs. Chesney's perfume. Then I would prance around like Sir Lancelot with a lance, and she would have to run me down before she could close the windows again.

We felt sorry for her, and were not really unkind. We tried to tell people. We played nursery rhymes with her week after week and then we'd take home report cards that said we were getting A's in arithmetic, history, spelling, and so on. We never looked into an arithmetic book all the time she was there. The break came when Chuck Dinsmore brought a tank to school.

The word "tank" was then a new one. The old Lombard log-hauler was a Maine invention and product, used in the woods to haul sled-trains of timber over iced roads. It was steam driven, and used hinged and cleated lugs that rolled around the gears, rather than wheels. The British swiped the idea for an armored war machine, and to keep the purpose secret from German intelligence they referred to the things as "tanks." Presumably the Germans thought they were some kind of a water tank, and when the machine first appeared in battle it was a total surprise. But long before this we'd been making "Lombards" out of a thread spool, and when we saw the pictures of tanks in the paper we began calling them tanks. We'd run a rubber band through the spindle-hole of a spool, and a little stick trailed out behind to make it go. We used paraffin wax to lubricate the spool, and if we cut notches in the rims of the spool with our jackknives the things would climb right up over a book and keep going. Wind up the rubber band, and you had a tank. Or a Lombard. Then Secretary Potter produced a refinement. He got one of the big shoemaker-thread spools from the shop, and cut a rubber band out of a 30 x 3½ innertube, and he had a magnificent tank that would run the whole length of the livery stable and climb right up the manure pile. This was the kind Chuck brought to school and set off down the aisle.

It took Mrs. Chesney right off her feet, rammed into the front wall to bounce off and go under a radiator, and it lay there churning its notches against a pipe until the elastic ran down. Mrs. Chesney pulled it out and was entranced. The next day we all made tanks in school and fought battles all over the place. Some of the girls were uninterested, but she pepped them up by saying the home folks must support the boys at the front. Secretary Potter heard how his playful artifact had assumed titanic educational proportions, and he began speaking his piece. Parents who hadn't listened to us began paying attention to what Secretary Potter said, and the school committee woke up. They eased Mrs. Chesney into the state hospital, and with only one week to go to Washington's Birthday vacation we had a new teacher. She threw away two wastebaskets of perfume bottles as her first task, and then she looked up at us and said, "You've had a regrettable experience. Regrettable. I shall try every way I know how to make it up to you — shall we go ahead, now, together?"

We did, but the next March the town reelected the same tired old school board, and in turn renamed the same old fuddy-dud superintendent. Years after ward when my own children would come home from school and talk about teachers, I used to think of Mrs. Chesney and I would listen to them. Sometimes I couldn't do much but listen, but Mrs. Chesney taught me to do that. And plug ratholes.

THE LOST CANNON

SOMEHOW, sometime, somebody is going to find the old Civil War cannon our town always shot off when midnight turned for the Fourth of July. It hasn't been seen now for well over a half-century. Before Joe Davis died he whispered, "It's in a cellar, but I don't remember which . . ." and the cannon was then so long gone that hardly anybody knew what he was talking about. Well greased and wrapped in burlap, the cannon is safe, wherever it is. Do you suppose some latter-day owner has expensively remodeled that old house, and has cemented the old dirt floor of the cellar without knowing what was under it?

In our town park you will see two cannon, flanking the stock statue (No. 52 in the catalog) of a Boy in Blue. Carved in myopic granite, the soldier stares down South Street as if anticipating an invasion from that direction, and the two cannon stand in perpetual readiness beside him. A pyramid of cannon balls is beside each. After the Civil War, when towns began erecting memorials to the heroes of Antietam and Appomattox, the granite industry sent salesmen around with catalogs showing the various statues that were ready. Our town selected No. 52. Then the War Department in Washington made cannon available to round out the sentimental gesture. As soon as the cannon were in place little beds of petunias and geraniums were prepared, and every Memorial Day the exercises would pause close by for the reading of the Gettysburg Address.

The cannon came by train. From surplus artillery the Army loaded flatcars, chaining the pieces securely, and the Boston & Maine railroad delivered a whole trainload to the Maine Central, which delivered them town by town along the line. The train paused in our town one summer afternoon, and a crew was waiting to unload the pair of cannon meant for us. And while this crew was busy at one end of the train a bunch of boys was just as busy at the other, tipping a third cannon off into the bushes. They were around the bend of the track, by the gristmill, and nobody could see them. The train pulled out, heading north. That night this third cannon was dismantled and dispersed. It would be sticky to have an unauthorized War Department cannon on hand, and shortly some town upstate was going to begin looking for one it didn't get. That winter the parts of the cannon were hidden under hay in various barns around town, and they weren't assembled again until the night before the next Fourth of July.

In stealth it was put together, and on the stroke of midnight it was touched off. Everybody was much astonished, and as barefoot citizens bounced their heels at bedside the houses shook and the hills re-echoed. It was a vast success. Then the boys took the cannon apart again and hid it out again. One year later it appeared again, and after that it settled into a tradition. The boys who tipped it off the train were growing older, and they began bringing their sons around to help.

Now one year, just for fun, a bunch of boys and men from the waterfront "captured" the cannon. Before the villagers could take it down and hide it after firing, a rude sally was made by superior numbers, and the gun was stolen. A year later, when the waterfront boys brought it out the villagers tried to steal it back. So a feud built up, and it didn't matter much which side had the cannon because it always got fired the night before the Fourth with equal zeal.

But one year the boys at the waterfront had a brilliant idea. Why bring the cannon out at all, and risk losing it? They got a couple of sticks of dynamite, capped and fused, and wrapped them well in wet oakum. Oakum was, and is, strands of hemp soaked with tar, and is pounded into the seams of boats for caulking. Joe Davis used to explain how they fixed this up, and he knew, because they swiped the dynamite and oakum from his father's shop. Thus wrapped tightly, the dynamite made a bomb, and it should sound very much like a cannon. So they never took the cannon out at all that year, but at midnight they set the dynamite bomb off on top of Weston's Hill. For a number of years the villagers would trot around trying to find the cannon when there wasn't any cannon.

During all this the cannon was buried in the chip piles at the shipyard, and after a few years those who knew where it was felt it needed some care. They dug it out, cleaned it, coated it with the heavy grease used for launching ships, sewed it into pieces of burlap and sailcloth, and laid it away in the dirt of "somebody's" cellar. If Joe Davis could have remembered . . . It's still there, of course, but where?

The bomb went off every year after that, and it was some time before word got around that the cannon itself had been retired. When they blew up Massy Coffin the fun sort of went out of it. They didn't mean to blow him up, of course. He was then a reasonably young man, but he already had second sight and could tell the future. He wore "plain-people" clothes, and with his black hat and black beard he looked older than he was. He considered himself a disciple, but was also believed harmless. When he went into a trance and told your fortune he would couch his remarks in double-talk, so you never knew if he had foretold the truth or not, but you were afraid he had. He was pleasantly regarded around town, and nobody ever thought of abusing him. So on this lovely night of the third of July he had gone up on Tory's Hill, which was something like the Mount of Olives to him, and he was having a trance there all by himself when the boys from the waterfront came along to set off their bomb. They didn't see Massy, all black in the dark under the trees. They lit the fuse and withdrew about a hundred yards to watch, and they didn't know Massy was there until the thing went off.

The flash revealed him sitting on a stump right beside the bomb. Massy came down off Tory's Hill like a Joseph Smith returning to Palmyra. The firmament had opened and the Glory of God burst forth. With his whiskers full of pine needles and bits of oakum Massy told of the beautiful revelation which had just come to him. Chariots of angels had coursed the skies, and flashes of God's wrath urged sinners to repent.

As time ran along Massy's vision grew and grew, and everybody agreed his experience had augmented his previous tendencies. It was kind of too bad. The bombs were never exploded again. Massy used to wander about selling cucumbers and tomatoes, and if you bought anything he would throw in a free trance. He would describe, once again, the magnificence of the Opening of the Doors of Heaven, and the loud report. Indeed, there came a time when Massy was still telling about it, and nobody knew any more to what he referred. And meantime up country is a one-cannon town where the stone soldier stares steadily south — as if looking for his other gun. I suppose if anybody ever finds it, and touches it off on the Glorious Fourth, those who hear it will think it's a sonic boom.

THE NET PROFIT

D EMOCRATS and foreigners could be counted on
your fingers in those days, and we had four of
each. It may have been three of the other, because
Nigger Charlie Murchison had been around longer
than either the natives or the Republicans. He was
dark, very dark, of skin, but probably was neither
Negro nor Murchison. His folks had come ashore
from the outside islands long ago. A man once asked
our Maine State Library for information about these
outside islands and their people, and he was told
there was nothing important on file — we keep our
dirty linen back and throw the fame at Myles Standish and Christopher Columbus. Charlie's people
were probably here before 1500, and the blood in
his cold, clam-digger's hands was a combination of
everything that ever buccaneered the North Atlantic
fisheries. It was said he could speak Portuguese. He
spoke English well, with a flourish that made him
sound like a Gothic novel. Charlie never discrim-
inated against us.

Then we had a German. During World War he got heckled some, not much, but he was from Pennsylvania and didn't know any more about the Vaterland than we did. The other two were a Swede named Sorenson and a French Canadian named Pete Renault, which he spelled and pronounced Reno. Other than this, ours was a pure Scots-Irish-English community — which is about as mixed-up as anybody needs. In the American Revolution we had been Loyalists, and in the Civil War we were about fifty-fifty for and ag'in. Ours are the hardest people in the world to tag with pat definitions and the easiest for strangers to mis-assess.

Before I took to the gravel business I used to make a little hay every summer, and there was always a job in the field. We put up two kinds of hay — to feed and to ship. The farmers packed away hay to feed out to their own stock, then we had dealers who pressed hay and sold it in the cities. I preferred to work for the farmers. The shippers were drivers, and didn't have to be so fussy about what they cut or how it was made. If they could get a wire around it and have it weigh out about right, it was hay. They didn't bale it until fall and winter, so both kinds went into the mows loose. Except for horse rakes and mowers we didn't have any machinery. Some barns had a track-fork unloader, some didn't. The farmers might not pay so much as the shippers, but they fed us, and we had to carry a dinner when we worked for the shippers. There is no hardship to eating a haymaker's dinner out on a farm.

So one year Sorenson and Reno entered into a partnership to cut hay. After each got his own hay in they joined up and began cutting and making small fields for village folks who still kept a horse. Because they were oddities, or foreigners, they had a little trouble getting hands, so when I applied they were delighted. Some of my friends thought I was crazy working for the foreigners. My father told me, "Sorensen will pay you if he handles the money; if Reno handles it, watch out. If they don't pay you the first week, don't go back the second."

Sorensen was lank and wiry, slow to respond to anything, methodical, and always looked grave before he laughed at anything. He didn't have much to say. Pete was bald as an egg, roly-poly, and he laughed at anything and everything whether it was funny or not. I never saw him look grave. He was built close to the ground, short-legged, and wore his pants well turned up at the cuffs. Although laundered, his shirts showed the sweat marks where his suspenders crossed. When Sorensen pushed his pitchfork into a bundle of hay and lifted it onto the rack he would just lift, but when Reno did it he would make a great grunt. Sorensen would lift as much as Reno. I was their one and only haymaker — nobody else came around.

Up to the time I broke my arm, I enjoyed it. Sorensen was grateful that I came to work, and took time to teach me some tricks. I was slight and wanted muscle, so he showed me how to get the tines into the hay to advantage. And he taught me to fix things. Most Maine farmers wait for the wheel to drop off before they fix the nut, but Sorensen always foresaw as much as he could. He greased the rack wheels every morning. Pete was more hearty with me, but Pete was hearty with everybody. He would greet me with, "Fine morning!" and then go, "Har, har, har!" If a tug snapped on a harness, Pete would go, "Har, har, har!" A horse would stop in the field to urinate and we'd hear Pete talking to him and going, "Har, har, har!"

Monday and Tuesday things went well. Wednesday it rained. Pete spent the rainy day assuaging the great disappointment he had with the weather, and he came to work Thursday as tight as a billygoat and barely able to stand up. He had brought reinforcements, and he laid the jug in the shade. Sorensen upbraided him and Pete said, "Har, har, har!" It is not possible to show in type the unmerciful defoliation a French-Canadian of Pete's time could wreak on Mother English, even if sober. Unless one has some knowledge of Habitant Québec any imitation will fail.

"You tink I no bon, eh?" Pete said, more or less.

"Ay tank yew ban trink awl-together too-oo strong-g-g-g," said Sorensen.

"She's strong," said Pete, poking his right bicep and almost knocking himself down.

"Vee got vork to do," said Sorensen.

Sorensen and I turned the hay, and while Pete made some pretense of helping he circled a good bit close to his jug. Sorensen discussed the evils of drink as we worked. "Vun trink is goo-ood vunce in a vile," he said. At noon Pete drank a hearty lunch and when he was quite finished he arose, beat his chest, and announced in all directions that he was about to begin raking. He was three times drunker than anybody else I've ever seen drunk, for his kind of raisin-larded cider doesn't do any fooling around. Sorensen and I laid back under a tree and watched Pete harness his horse.

For raking Pete was using Lily-Louise, a retired racetrack veteran still able to make time, and still frisky when she saw a bit coming. But Pete won, and I held Lily-Louise's bridle while Pete found the seat of the horserake. I had to jump back when he clouted her over the rump with the ends of the reins and put her into a standing start. Pete and Lily-Louise raked hay at State Fair speed. Now, the teeth on those old trip-rakes operated off the wheels. When you depressed the foot lever a rod locked in and the teeth were lifted up to drop the load. At the top point the rod kicked itself out and gravity brought the teeth down so they'd gather up a new load. Well, at high speed gravity didn't work that fast and the teeth never came back down to the ground again. Pete raked all afternoon with his teeth clicking around in mid-air. This perplexed him, as he found he was raking places he had already raked, and it drove Lily-Louise in a faster clip. She didn't like the noise, and Pete didn't help any by going, "Har, har, har!" all the time. There wasn't a thing Sorensen and I could do except wait for Pete to fall off, which he did after a while, and then I ran Lily-Louise down. I walked her around for a while to cool her, and then tied her in the shade. We put Pete in the shade, too, and he and Lily-Louise were still there when we came to work Friday morning. On Saturday they were gone, though, and Sorensen and I did all the haying, and when it came time to pay me he said Pete was handling the money.

I knew my father was going to say, "I told you so," and he did. "You've learned your lesson," he said. That's worth something." But I thought things over, and Sunday morning I went back to help Sorensen. I felt sorry for him. He had hay down and he needed help. "If I don't show up, he's stuck," I told my father. "If you show up, you're stuck," he said. But I showed up. Sorensen was mighty glad to see me. Ordinarily, we didn't hay on Sunday, but Pete's bender had crowded things. Then on Monday, about four in the afternoon, I fell off the rack and twisted my left wrist into a jack-straw jumble that Dr. Gilchrist spent all night weeding out. I was done haying for that summer. When it first happened, I remember how amazed I was that my hand looked wrong-side up on my arm, but it didn't seem to hurt much. This puzzled me. I had heard that people badly wounded will stare stupidly at their injuries, but I wasn't staring stupidly — I was looking with deep interest. Why didn't it hurt more? Sorensen came over and said, "Ay tank you bro-oak yewer arm; I heard it cra-ack!"

Dr. Gilchrist when he came agreed with Sorensen. I took my arm home, and the doctor came there to set it. I remember my mother cried when she found out what happened, and I said, "Why are you crying? It's my arm!" But she didn't stop. Dr. Gilchrist was cutting the top off an ether can as he rounded the doorway into my presence, and he said, "It's all right, Laddie-boy; everything's all right — I love to set broken bones!" He did a good job. And when he got through my arm was hurting, all right.

I had, of course, earned no money from my hay-making with Sorensen and Reno. Dr. Gilchrist charged my father twenty-five dollars for setting my arm, and tape, gauze and ether ran the total up to $28.35. Dad never confronted me with a financial statement, but I knew how he was thinking, and he didn't have to. After a few days the pain began to wear off, and after a few more my arm began to itch under the cast. Worse than that, my unwashed arm began to stink. I had an awful time living in my own smell. I told Dad about then that I was suffering well over the $28.35, and he patted me and said, "The past is prologue." And yet, resigned as I was, I still had a feeling Sorensen was all right and would prove it.

But it was Pete Reno who came around one afternoon. I was making the most of my arm, so I did a lot of sitting around with it. They didn't ask me to do anything around the house, so I didn't. I was sitting reading in the front room when Pete arrived — marching in as if he had been there a thousand times and held the mortgage on the place. "Har, har, har!" he said. "You bus' de h'arm! Dat's too bad; I verree sorree."

Then he spoke the magic words: " 'Ow much h'I h'owe you?"

I knew exactly how much he h'owed me. It was Monday to Monday with Wednesday out, and half of fourteen dollars would be seven dollars. Pete owed me seven dollars. I said, "It was Monday to Monday with Wednesday out."

Pete hauled a leather wallet from his hip pocket, and it was salty from years of sweat. The fold fell open, and he had a flock of bills bigger than anything I'd seen except in a bank. He fingered out two tens and a five and handed them to me. "You tink dis h'all right?" he asked.

I started to protest, but Pete said, "No, you tak heem — she's you h'earn h'it. You h'earn h'every damn cent. I won't 'ave no broken h'arm for ten tams dat much. Beside, dat Soren-sen, he tol' me you catch my Lily-Louise. Good boy to catch 'orse lak dat!"

I distinctly remember that Pete did not har-har-har with this speech.

He was good faller, dat Pete. I gave the twenty-five dollars to my father and he made a pretext of applying it to the doctor's bill, but it turned up in my savings account afterwards, and I suppose I frittered it away when I got to college. Later that afternoon I was one-handing some scratch grain to my hens when Sorensen came into the henhouse.

He wanted to know how much he owed me.

"Pete paid me already," I said.

He said, "Pee-eet pa-ay his sha-are; I pa-ay mine!"

He gave me twenty-five dollars.

So I netted $21.65 by breaking my arm, and I found out that foreigners aren't the worst people in the world.

THE ICEMAN DEPARTETH

PEDDLING ice was considered good summer training for football heroes.   There was also a whisper that any good iceman got seduced four and five times a morning by housewives. I never played football, and I very seldom got seduced, but when people say, "How would you like to be the iceman?" I can truthfully answer, "I *was* the iceman!" At my fighting weight of a hundred and fifteen pounds I toted ice all one summer. My uncle was the ice dealer in town, and this is known as nepotism.

This uncle was already aware that mechanical refrigeration was on the way. They had it for cold-storage plants, and he could envision the household model. In fact, he tried to tie up dealerships for Maine, but nobody was ready to do business then and the idea went by the board. But he'd say, "The day is coming," and continue to cut and peddle pond ice. Things started at six-thirty A.M. when we fed the horses, shined harness and greased the cart. If tools were dull we touched them up. After the horses finished their oats we'd water them, hitch them into the cart, and drive two miles to the icehouse.

There we dug the great cakes of ice out of their insulating hay and sawdust, wrestled them out into the cart, and tiered them up for peddling. That same year my uncle bought his first truck, a Lippert-Stuart that had about the same power as a Casco one-lunger, but he used that for wholesale deliveries and I didn't get to ride on it much. My uncle believed that the icecart was his show window, so he kept it painted and used heavy horses. It was the sharpest rig in town, and it gave me a majestic feeling to sit up and ride along. My job was to take ten- and fifteen-cent pieces into the homes. This wasn't hard work, and I could handle a twenty-five-cent piece, but we didn't have too many iceboxes in town that would hold that size. Ice retailed for one-half cent a pound but we seldom weighed a piece and for ten cents you'd get about thirty pounds.

The morning I went to work I wore cotton shirt and pants, because it was warm summer weather, and my Lion Brand boots. Ned Wheeler, who was my boss on the icecart, shook his head and said I'd have to get some woolen clothes. The very first cake of ice I carried told me why. If you can remember "iceman's pants" you will recall that no other profession ever wore such heavy garb in hot weather. Once a cake of ice has swung against thin cotton overalls and the calf of your leg learns about it, you will see the reason. When you lift a cake of ice to fit it into the top of a box and the drip caresses your belly, you know how Winkelried felt when he was stabbed. I took time out to go to Bean's and get some iceman pants. The wool absorbed the cold and the drip, and I was all right.

The average icebox turned out to be one of man's better achievements. Or, let us say, woman's. The thing they did most of all was wrap the cake of ice in newspaper so it wouldn't melt away so fast. Since the melting process is what cools the box, this reduced efficiency. Because efficiency was reduced they couldn't keep milk and butter down below, so they'd move these things up into the top, with the ice. So, on top of the wet, soggy, slimy, sticking newspaper the iceman would find cucumbers, cream jugs, and things as wonderfully surprising as a mess of eels. I actually found a dead cat there one time — the lady was keeping it cool until she got a chance to bury it.

Whatever was there had to be lifted out, the new ice inserted, and the old worn-out piece chipped to fit around the new. Then there was no place for the cucumbers, tomatoes, etc. We would find ten cents in a little dish, or with charge customers we'd

reach up with the stub of a lead pencil and write
10¢ on the card tacked to the wall. One woman
somehow got an extra one of these cards one time,
and she cheated my uncle for years. The last day of
every month she'd switch cards, and put up one that
showed eighty cents. Then she'd keep the card and
put it back up the next time. All she ever paid was
eighty cents. I figured out what she was doing, and
I began dating the card. My uncle was very happy
when I told him about this.

I remember one woman Ned and I hated. She was
"nasty-neat." Her shed floor was always newly washed,
and she'd stand there and tell us not to drip on it.
A 32° cake of ice carried in 80° summer weather is
going to drip. But she made it even worse. She
wanted her ice clean, and she would set a pan of
water on the back steps that we were supposed to
slosh over the cake before we lugged it in. We had
a big whiskbrush on the cart, and we carefully dusted
the ice anyway, but this wasn't good enough for
Mrs. Ritch-Bitch, which is what Ned called her. The
pan of water would sit in the hot sun all morning,
and when we sloshed it over the cake you could see
the ice melt away. We'd lug in a fifty-cent piece,
slosh it, and put a ten-center in her box. Being
clean cost her a lot of money. One day Ned had a
wonderful idea. He found a cake of ice that had a
horse-bun frozen in it. Horses pulled the grooving
tools on the icepond during the harvest, and this
oddity had been created and preserved. You could
look through the clear, smooth ice and see this con-

gealed defecation in its original perfection, like the fly in the amber. The ice magnified it a little. When Ned found it he called right out, "There's a piece of ice for Mrs. Ritch-Bitch!" We pushed it around in the cart all morning, saving it, and we showed it to about everybody and told them what we planned to do with it, but when we got to Mrs. Ritch-Bitch's house we didn't have courage enough to go through with it. But give her credit — she had one of the few iceboxes that didn't stink when we opened the cover, and she never wrapped newspapers around her ice. I always wondered why she didn't wait and wash her shed floor after the iceman came.

Women would wait for the iceman to help them with little chores. Invitations to the boudoir might sometimes have been welcome, but all we got was, "Oh, while you're here, would you empty the pan for me?" Some ice chests were piped with a drain, but most of them had a pan underneath to catch the water. Nobody ever emptied this when it was half full, but everybody waited until it began to run over. Then they'd say, "Don't spill it!" They'd say, "See if you can unstick this drawer for me, will you?" One woman asked me to mail a package at the post office, and if it cost more to add the difference to her ice bill. One time I was gone over-long, and when I came back to the cart Ned said, "She putting out a little this morning?" I said, "I was getting the baby's thumb unstuck from a toothpowder can." It was true. She said, "Oh, see if you can help me — Clarice has her thumb stuck!"

There was one young mother with a flock of babies, and she lived up on a third floor where a flock of babies must have been a nuisance. She was pretty, I thought, and as far as I know virtuous, if prolific. Being pretty, and being on a third floor, she was automatically good grist for iceman jokes. I carried a chunk of ice up one morning, climbed over the erector sets and tinker toys in the hall, opened the chest, took out the hamburg, butter and head of lettuce, removed the wet paper, lifted out the old ice, inserted the new, fitted the old back, finally closed the cover, and reached up to write *10¢* on the card. She appeared and said, "I didn't want any ice today."

I said, "Your card's up." This was a card the customer could put in the front window to let the iceman know from the street how big a piece to bring in. It had *10, 25, 35* and *50* on the four edges, and whichever was up was what we lugged in. I don't remember anybody ever had a 50. That would have been a hundred pounds, and I couldn't have lifted it. Anyway, I said, "Your card's up."

She said, "I forgot to take it down."

So I retrieved my ice, put back the hamburg, butter and lettuce, erased the *10¢* on the card, climbed out over the tinker toys, and got back to the cart.

"What'd she do, give you a free ride this morning?" asked Ned.

"I said, "She didn't want any ice."

Ned said, "Her card's up!"

I said, "She forgot to take it down."

By this time we were on the seat of the cart, and

what Ned said scared the horses. They ran away. "The bahstids got the bits in their teeth!" he yelled, and I could see that it was so. The cart was bouncing eight feet off the ground as they slatted it around, and they had no intention of stopping. They turned down Mill Hill, came up Railroad Avenue, coursed Mechanic, hit School, and came back to Main again. Secretary Potter ran out and threw his arms up and stopped them. I wouldn't have gone in front of those horses for anything, but Secretary stood there with his arms spread wide, and they stopped for him. "Whoa, now — whoa," he whispered, and the huge beasts turned softie and quit.

"What happened to cause that?" asked Secretary Potter.

Ned said, "Well, you see, this damn Fernald woman leaves her card up, but she don't want no ice . . ."

". . . Oh, skip it," concluded Ned. "You wouldn't understand."

"I sure as hell don't," said Secretary Potter.

September came, and unseduced I went back to school. My uncle bought me a belt for my pants, kind of a bonus, and said I'd done all right. He said, "Don't plan on making it a life's work. Before you set up housekeeping they'll have electric ice chests." I think I didn't believe him, but he was right. Once in a while, in a reminiscent mood, I will burst forth with the words of an old song Ned and I used to sing as we went along on the canopied seat of my uncle's deluxe icecart. As I remember them, they went like this:

Oh, it's nice to be the iceman,
And so is your old iceman,
  Oh, how about a piece of ice today?
It's only a quarter,
You know that you orta,
  Hurry up, before it melts away!
Yes, ma'am, yes ma'am,
Not on your linole-am,
No ma'am, no ma'am,
Giddyap, Napole-am.
  It's nice today, Lady —
  Some ice today, Lady?
Oh, lady, be good to me!

THE ECONOMICS

THE old lumbering, seafaring and granite-quarrying days had gone, and our local economy had become the shoe shop. I never worked in one, and may be a poor one to talk, but making shoes always seemed to me to be a mighty poor way to get along. Year after year our respected local citizens rose before breakfast and went to bed after supper, and lived lives of dreary desperation. They made shoes all day in inefficient, unpleasant surroundings, at pittances, and the chief intellectual height was to worry about being "laid off." When orders for shoes dropped off, our town buttoned its pockets and waited things out.

The big trouble with a shoe factory was, and is, that you don't have to be over-bright to run one. Oh, there are specialty shops and exceptions, but when you get down on the straightaway the competition isn't intellectual. Even plumbers and morticians hold conventions and talk things over for the good of the order, but the first successful shoe-factory convention is yet to be held. A shoe-factory owner plugs along thinking nobody else is around. For some few there is fun in designing, or creating a style that catches on, but mostly it's a humdrum business worth avoiding. In late years as politics put the skids under shoes it has become fashionable to stand up and howl as if you'd been insulted — but whatever happens to the shoe business, the shoe business has asked for it. Sometimes when dwindling economies catch up with towns they say, "Oh, if we could only get a shoe factory!" I wouldn't wish it on any town. It does something to the people, and no payroll is big enough to make up for it.

If you work in a shoe shop, ten thousand others can do your job just as well as you can. The man who owns the shop doesn't care about you, and would just as soon have the other ten thousand. The finances of operation aren't much, and if things get sticky he can move along. Banks go good for leather, and you can borrow on an option to meet payrolls. The United Shoe Machinery Corporation will bring in equipment on lease and rental. Just as I was getting big enough to notice things our principal shoe factory closed. People who had worked there for years were told on Saturday there would be no work on Monday. They had helped make the owner rich, and he didn't care one hoot.

The town tried a bootstrap project — they sold stock, bought the building, and looked for a tenant. There was never the slightest thought of getting anything except a shoe factory! One man showed up and said he'd like to start a molded-pulp products factory, and he showed them a toilet seat he'd made. It looked like porcelain, but it was wood pulp with baked enamel. Instead of getting excited, the town began calling the place the privy-shop, and in time the fellow was ridiculed out of town. That his little idea finally grew into the Keyes Fibre Company, with mills all over, but none in our town, causes no local chagrin. When you think shoes, you don't reach beyond that. Everybody was happy when a man said he would make shoes in the place.

He did. He didn't have a nickel when he came, but he made out, and soon he was rich, and our people were still wondering when they'd be laid off.

Over the years our town made every kind of foot-wear there ever was. One of our shops, indeed, made the famous Congress boot — it had an elastic side and no buttons or lacings. Long after even Congress stopped wearing them our little shop kept on making them, and nobody there was bright enough to change to a changed market, and everybody was astonished when the place failed up. One shop for a time made men's and boys' shoes that retailed nationwide in a chain store for four dollars a pair. The pasteboard box they came in would wear longer, and I think the situation pointed up the local problem. A man ought to be doing something he can take pride in. Our town belittled these shoes all the way, and that isn't good. I have an idea I was the only person in town who ever wore a pair of these shoes — I used to buy rejects for twenty-five cents a pair from

Chester Brawn, who ran the boxing department. I wore a ten-D, and whenever a pair came along with crooked seams Chester would save them for me. One time I went in and Chet said, "I ain't got none your size — but wait a minute, I'll have a pair damaged." I had dozens of pairs of them, all colors and styles, and I'd wear them a few times before they came apart. Every month or so a man would come and make Chester an offer for all the damaged pairs he had on hand, and he'd sell them in the city somewhere. I suppose he made more money than anybody.

Our town did not wear the shoes our town made. This forever bothered me as a boy. That, and the unstable nature of shoe-shop gossip. Shoe workers knew more things that weren't so than anybody. This could range from international incidents down to a grammar school girl who was going to have a baby. The shoe shop would lament the death of some respected citizen and take up a collection to buy flowers, and he wouldn't be dead at all. But sometimes somebody would die, and the shoe shop wouldn't know it until they read it in the paper.

Possibly for the better, some of this changed when labor unions ascended. The piecework pittances and the horrid working conditions of a shoe shop gave the union organizers a wonderful place to start. The first factory ever organized by the CIO in Maine was one of our shoe shops. They had a list of grievances a rod long, including the complaint that there was no toilet paper in the retiring rooms. People used to steal rolls of paper and take them home, so management stopped putting paper around. The union was successful, so now people could steal toilet paper again. They had big mass meetings and parades, and people who had been stealing toilet paper demanded their rights. I'm sorry, but it's hard for me to get sentimental over shoe shops.

Most of the boys and girls in my class came from shoe-shop people, and most of them had little to look forward to except shoemaking. The girls studied typing and shorthand, with the idea of avoiding stitching and lasting, and working in the office. "There's nothing else to do here," was the lament. Mine was a far better than average class, and I think we lifted ourselves away from the bootstraps rather well. Two of us went to college and finished; several of us went on to higher schools and didn't finish. Somewhere along the line I think we reached beyond our grasp, and perhaps that's what schooling's for.

Diddy Dinsmore did that, too. Diddy was a shoemaker, and it didn't suit him. So he opened a cobbler shop on Main Street, and he repaired shoes for shoemakers. This always seemed pat to me. His little place smelled like a shoe shop, and he had the same machines that you find in a shoe shop. But Diddy had opinions of his own, and he didn't worry about being laid off. There was one thing he did that set him apart — he made shoes that he wore himself. He wouldn't make them for other people. He said shoemakers couldn't afford to buy the kind he made.

THE FOURTH CAN

O<small>NE</small> year we had so much snow they closed the shoe shops and everybody shoveled out the trolley car tracks. It's pretty hard to tell people now about our trolley cars, but there was a time you could leave New York City and ride all the way to Old Town, Maine, on electrics. When I was a baby my mother and father brought me home from Boston one time on trolley cars — we stayed overnight at Portsmouth, New Hampshire, and started out again the next day. Our little trolley car line was only twenty miles long, but it connected on both ends with other lines that, in turn, connected. True, we had steam trains through town, too, and the prices were about the same, but we liked the trolley cars if we were going to the city to shop, because they took us right to the stores. And our trolley cars would stop anywhere, as a bus does now, while the steam cars made but one stop in each town. The trolley cars ran every hour.

The day the town turned out to shovel the tracks was one of the prettiest we ever had in Maine. The no'theast blizzard had howled for three days and two nights, and then the wind had turned westerly and the sky was bright. Milt Dill had floundered a team around the village, and for our purposes in those days the roads were "broken." But drifts ran across the gables of houses where the wind had struck just right, and the electric car tracks were hopelessly lost. Bill Libby was the motorman on the electric snowplow, and he hadn't much more than got the thing out of the carbarn. The big wedge-shaped blade just rammed itself into the snow, and then the wheels would spin on the rails and Bill couldn't back the thing up. All that first day after the storm Bill kept trying, but there was just too much snow.

The second day they closed the shops and every man in town was there with a shovel. Bill would ram the plow into a drift and then they would dig him out. He'd back the plow up, ram it again, and get stuck again. When the blade hit the drift, snow would burst fifty feet into the air, and it was beautiful. When they got the tracks all clear you could ride the whole twenty miles and not see a thing out the trolley car windows but the banks of snow.

Through town, for about a mile and a half, the tracks ran up the middle of Main Street. Thus we now had eight and ten feet of snow along the street, with the straight-down gorge of the trolley tracks along the center. Naturally, lacking a better place, people walked on the trolley tracks, and whenever a trolley came along they couldn't climb up the side and get out of the way. So for a few days a trolley car would arrive in town and slowly make its way with fifteen or twenty people walking along ahead of it trying to find a place they could climb up. Then Bill Libby rigged a wide plank on his snowplow, caught out at right angles with a cable, and he began beveling off the canyon of snow. Every time he ran by he'd push back a little, and he spent a whole day going back and forth in the village. When we got through, Main Street was V-shaped, starting high up on the trees along the sidewalk and sloping down to the tracks. We could climb up now, but all winter the sleighs and teams would try to get out of the way of the cars and would slide back.

In the village square there was a turn-out, where the hourly cars met and passed, one for each direction. In the early days of the line these cars would be full of people, but by my time the business had dwindled. I used to ride on them when I'd be the only passenger, and if Henry Walsh was the motorman I'd cling to a steel post alongside him and talk all the way. Henry was the only motorman who ever let me run the car, and the first time I threw the handle over so it just about spun the wheels off. But he showed me how to gain on the rheostat slowly and after that I could run the car as well as he did.

When we played baseball "away" we always went by trolley. And if by chance we caught a little money ahead we could take the trolley and spend Saturdays in the city and see the Jefferson Players and eat supper at the Oriental Restaurant — but we were in trouble if we didn't catch the last car home. All our school parties had to end in time for the trolley children to catch the last car — quite a few who lived on the outskirts along the line came and went by the cars. If I was squiring a girl and she missed the last car I'd have to walk her home, explain to her mother, and then return to the village in my own uninteresting company. It was never worth it. All those old trolley lines were connected with a pleasure park, known simply as a "trolley park." With us it was Casco Castle, but Riverton, Merrymeeting Park, and Lake Grove were others within reach. These parks had zoos, bathing beaches, amusements, picnic and dining facilities, and on good summer Sundays the open cars would carry crowds back and forth — the trolley ticket including the amusement park fee. We used to see some wonderful baseball games at these parks, with each team usually featuring a pitcher named Jones or Smith who was really a big-leaguer having a day off from the Braves or Red Sox.

These parks usually wound up their programs with fireworks, and a big piece would go off and say "Good

Night" just before time for the last car. We'd come home pooped. These trolley lines made money for their investors for many years, but after automobiles got common the business tapered off. One by one they threw in the sponge, and then there would be a big Public Utilities Commission hearing to decide on abandonment. People who hadn't ridden the cars for years would come in and protest that they were indispensable. Motormen who rode lonesome miles in empty cars found they had a lot of friends. Most of the rails had been taken up by the thirties. Only those who rode on these Toonerville Trolleys know how a hot motor smelled on a long upgrade. It is a distinctive aroma and one you never forget.

There was one trolley story worth setting down. One of the hotels down at Bath had a fancy man who used to ride our electric cars through town and fetch back the booze from Portland. This went on for years and was a constant source of joy to parched tongues in our area. He would ride up to Brunswick and then shift over to our line, and at the end of our line would shift again for the rest of the route. When he got to Portland he would go to the waterfront where he had a source of supply. For this errand he had a suitcase with three specially made tin cans in it — one for whiskey, one for rum and one for gin. When he got the cans filled he would start home on the trolleys. It took him all day to make the round trip, and on the way home his suitcase was heavy. Instead of lugging it inside the car he would leave it on the rear platform. This was not wholly so it wouldn't be in people's way — it was so he could disclaim ownership if a sheriff asked any questions. What tipped his hand was the regularity of his trips. He came and he went every Thursday. The motormen and conductors on our trolley line didn't need to have the roof fall on them.

One day they looked into his unprotected suitcase, and then the boys around the carbarn got a can to keep on the car the fancy man used. While the fancy man was up front reading his newspaper and looking like a respectable citizen, the conductor would open his suitcase and remove a small but adequate sample from each can — pouring all three samples indiscriminately into the fourth can provided by the boys in the carbarn. True, this created a mixture of whiskey, gin and rum, but up to a late hour no complaints have been registered. In those days you could take any given kind. As soon as this rapine had been accomplished the conductor would signal to the motorman, and the motorman would negotiate Mallett's Curve at a slow pace. This was so the conductor could lean down and set that fourth can into the bushes along Mallett's Curve. Some people used to wonder why the car went so slowly there, and always assumed it was a dangerous place in the rails. The fancy man, of coures, rode to the end of the line and got off — seeming not to notice that his load had been lightened.

For a great many years this trifling peccadillo was the principal fringe benefit to a carbarn job. The fancy man never let on he knew the difference — perhaps he felt safe passage was worth a tip. They said that years later somebody asked him if he ever found out who stole his booze on the trolley car, and he said, "I just have."

THE SPECIAL TEACHER

ONCE in a while in every school system they'll get a nasty man teacher who plays around with little girls. Then there'll be a big scandal about it and a lot of, "Well, I never's!" and they'll fire the teacher. My second year in high school we were much more fortunate — we had a lovely lady teacher who played around with little boys. Pudge Perkins always said it was the high spot in his education.

In those days the schools still went to some effort to teach, but the tail was beginning to wag the dog. Our only "special" teacher had been for music, but just lately manual training and domestic science had been added. The music teacher came once a week, but manual training and domestic science moved right in and had their rooms in the basement. At first most of the menfolks called manual training "sloyd," and domestic science was later changed to home economics. It didn't matter; they just meant a free period from studies. Then the town felt gen-

erous one March meeting and raised money to estab-
lish a physical training program. In due time a grad-
uate of Sargent School was hired to conduct it.
When this teacher turned out to be a female some
of the voters were surprised, and when she turned
out to be available Pudge Perkins was overjoyed. He
tumbled her on the fall strawride, and after that it
was open season. By the time the girl's principal talent was town gossip and the school board got to fire
her, the general subject of physical training was in
disrepute and the town meeting would have none of
it. It was years before the school superintendent
could think of some way to disguise it in the budget
so he could get it passed.

I suppose all these things are as stupid today as
they were then, but they have become established
by acceptance and the taxpayers' shrugs of so-what.
The music teacher was a dedicated crusader who
couldn't even play a piano, and she'd swing a little
stick to bring out our latent harmony. One music
teacher we had pushed Brahms and Mozart, and had
us sing a song she called "Joo-wan-night-ta." We
never had a glee club; we never sang a concert. But
once a week this special teacher would come in, our
regular teachers would disappear for an hour, and
we'd sing. The town paid her $600 a year and she
provided her own stick.

The manual training and the domestic science
teachers labored in a strange vineyard. They were
teaching, or trying to teach, certain arts and skills in
a town that was miles ahead of them. Girls who

helped their mothers in the kitchens every Saturday were taught to make cookies that used a quarter of an egg. And I remember the first day in manual training when the teacher walked around saying, "This is a saw; this is a plane; this is a bitstock . . ." The quarter-egg cookies are a fact. Four girls worked at one table, and they divided a one-egg recipe. Ours was a poultry town and eggs were plentiful. Indeed, when Mrs. Bunker heard that Carolyn was making quarter-egg cookies she sent a box of eggs to school. I suppose today a teacher with a can opener and a TV tray can teach home economics and not get chucked out, but it was different in our time.

One day the domestic science teacher came into the manual training room to see if we boys would make some curtain rods. The girls in the sewing class were making curtains for the domestic science room, and they needed hangers. Pudge Perkins and I went in to measure the windows, and after we made the rods we went back to put them up. I asked the manual training teacher where the centering punch was, and he said, "The what?" Every joiner's bench and every toolbox in town had a centering punch, but the school didn't. We looked in all the drawers and cupboards. A centering punch locates screwholes; so Pudge and I guessed at the screwholes, and then when the girls put the curtains up they had the pattern on the cloth upside down.

A few nights later we had visiting night for the parents and the new curtains attracted a lot of attention. All the mothers asked, "Why did you make them upside down?" and all the fathers said, "Why didn't you use a centering punch?"

But I was glad to take manual training, because I wanted to make a toolbox. When I did benchwork at home in the wintertime I had a cold barn to work in, and the steam-heated shop at school appealed to me. And I needed a toolbox. When I was twelve I made a birch canoe, and I found I liked to work with tools. The next year I made a moose-sled. So I was picking up odd tools here and there, with nothing to keep them in. We had no home-workshop power tools then, and neither did the school — but I did have some good chisels and bits, the saws and hammers, and I had a few planes and molders. I had also spoken to Mr. Porter, our lumberman, and asked him to keep an eye out for some good inch-and-a-quarter pine. He told me he had it seasoning in his loft. And I had the design and measurements. There had been a ship's carpenter from our town in the old days, named Bibber, and he had put in his time on long voyages making beautiful chests. They were of many sizes and of different kinds of lumber, but they all had the beautiful dovetailing that was a Brewer hallmark, and you could tell a Bibber Chest from all others. I had taken the dimensions off one I liked and now that I was studying manual training I was all ready to go.

But my manual training teacher said the big things would have to wait until we had mastered the rudiments and understood the uses of the various tools. So I drew a line with a square on a board and sawed the board off, and then I drew another line and sawed it off again. In this way I mastered the rudiments of the square and the saw. Then I learned to use the plane. I spent a good time gaining skill as a sandpaperer, and found out how to stain things walnut. Our manual training teacher was a great hand for walnut. By this time I was ready for work, so I made a tie rack. It was a lovely tie rack, stained walnut, and then I made some bookends. Every house in our town had some of these pine bookends at one time or another, and you would see them on front-room tables holding up the Bible and the novels of Winston Churchill. I made my bookends, and when the walnut stain was dry I took them home to my mother and she said, "Oh, goodie! Just what I've always wanted!"

The only good thing about those bookends was that they qualified me for making my toolchest. I went to see Mr. Porter and he tenderly handed the stock down from his loft. "You take your time," he said. "This is beautiful wood!" The smooth boards, without a knot, were more than beautiful. Mr. Porter, remembering that I had a chest in mind, watched the logs as they went through his mill, and one day he had the sawyer stop and set over to get me out just the right thickness. Those old trees are gone and we don't see logs like that any more. Mr. Porter liked boys, and took an interest in them, and I'm sure he scaled the boards down so I paid no more than cost. He took my money and said, "I'd like to see this chist when you git it done." And after I started away, carrying the pine, he called after me, "An' f'Gawd's sake, don't put no damn walnut stain to it!" When I did come to paint the finished chest some time later, I went back to let Mr. Porter advise me on a color. He suggested tobacco brown. "Only thing for a chist," he said. So my toolchest has always been tobacco brown.

But I didn't finish the chest in school. When June came I shoved the pieces into the back corner of the shop, and I pulled them out again in September. I worked on them all fall, and had the dovetailing all done and the corners tight. I had the trim mitered, but not attached, and I had the cover fitted but no hinges in place. I had the beckets rove, which proved to be a maneuver of much interest to the teacher, but I hadn't attached them. And about then I decided that manual training was wasting my time. I had French and physics going, and just when I was stewing over them the most I'd have to go to the basement and work on my chest. I could finish the chest at home, but I had to get French and physics in school. I went to the principal's desk and told him I thought my toolchest was interfering with my studies.

"Toolchest?" he said. "I didn't know they made anything down there except tie racks."

"And bookends," I said.

"How do you happen to be making a toolchest?" he asked. I said I had some tools at home and did quite a bit of carpenter work, besides making birch canoes, and I needed a toolchest. "I must see this," he said, and he went down to the manual training basement three steps at a time and was gone about half an hour. When he came back he called me to his desk and said he had arranged for me to drop manual training, unless perhaps I wanted to teach it, and that he expected to see me raise my grade in Latin next term. "I just got this college catalog in the mail," he said. "Perhaps you'd like to look it over at home tonight?"

So the next day I took my moose-sled to school and tied my toolchest on it for the ride home. My father happened to be looking out the kitchen window when I hove into view, and he said, "Good Lord! He's bringing home a cadaver in a casket!"

I finished the toolchest afterwards, and I've kept my tools in it ever since. Now and then somebody sees it and says, "Where did you ever get that lovely antique chest!" It is my chiefest souvenir from schoolday brushes with special teachers — but then, I never did get to take a physical training instructress on a class ride.

THE TROUT POOL

Tucked away in my fishing-tackle box is my hunting and fishing license. It is one of the original Maine licenses, and it cost me twenty-five cents. It is, it says, valid as long as I am a bona fide resident of Maine. Of course the state welched on these licenses long ago, and now we must renew every year at a much larger fee, but I have tucked this antique document into the box to wait for some young warden to ask for my license. He may never have seen one of these. Town Clerk Robert E. Randall made mine out, and he said he thought things had come to a pretty pass when a boy had to spend a quarter just to hunt and fish.

I didn't say so, but I didn't agree with him. I thought it was well worth a quarter, and at that time I possessed the greatest single piece of information available to an angler — I knew where the trout were. They were in the brook and pools just outside the village where the signs said, Public Water Supply — No Fishing.

In those days our town water wasn't very good. The system was owned by absentee private owners, and if a liquid appeared when a customer opened a faucet the contract had been fulfilled. The supply was Pumping Station Brook, which was fed by smaller brooks and puddles in quite a large drainage area. The liquid was nutritious and tasty, particularly in the fall when autumn leaves clogged the settling pools. A bathtub of warm water would smell like a bog of beavers. All this was absurd, because Maine was ever the land of sweet-flowing waters, and we could have had the best. But this did make for good fishing, and trout from the waterworks were fat.

One year Dr. Gilchrist chanced to remark that our town water wasn't fit to bathe in, and this touched off an idea for a float in the Fourth of July Parade. Some of the men put a bathtub on a wagon, and they had a hand pump that lifted water out of the tub and poured it back in again. They had steeped about three pounds of tea in the water, so it had a natural look. Up in the tub, naked as far as anybody could see, they had Baby Butch Hutchins — a big lubberly fellow of dubious origin and under-par mentality. As the float moved along a couple of men were pumping the water, and Baby Butch was scrubbing his back with a long-handled brush. Secretary Potter drove the horses. Over the bathtub was a sign that said, *Town Water System.* On one side of the wagon a big banner said, *Our Water Comes From A Dammed Brook.* On the other side it said, *One Bath In Our Water And You'll Never Take Another.* In truth, it was the only bath Baby Butch ever took. Not long after that there was a Public Utilities hearing, and the company was ordered to improve its quality, but by that time most of the tea had bleached off Baby Butch.

I made use of the waterworks in the meantime. I found that while the public was warned away the superintendent was using the flowage as his own private fish preserve. He'd go up every evening and start the pump running to fill the standpipe, and the standpipe would run over the top for about an hour and a half. On nights when it was unpleasant, or a thundershower had sent the trout down, the standpipe didn't run over at all. Izaak Walton says angling is the contemplative man's recreation, and I contemplated this oddity until I figured out an answer, and then I, too, went angling in the waterworks. I figured if anybody caught me there it would be the superintendent, and he wasn't in a position to get nasty. He never caught me. One night after some seasons I heard a twig snap and a man came down and said, "What are you doing here?" I started to say I was fishing, and then I said, "Probably what you're going to do." He gave me a long-winded explanation about how his dog had got onto a woodchuck, and he had come down to see if he'd caught him, and he was the only man I ever saw hunting a woodchuck with a fishpole.

I did my first fly-fishing there. One evening the trout were leaping all over the place, but my worm wasn't doing any business. Most people in those days said fly-fishing was a fancy-pants pursuit, and good old garden-hackle was tried and true. But I tied some hen-feather flies and caught trout when they wouldn't touch worms. I'd get one trout on a fly, and then the fly would fall apart. And I didn't have any fly-rod; I did my fly-casting with an alder pole. Once, on a worm, I caught a monstrous great eel in the waterworks pool, and this is the best argument I ever heard of for fly-fishing. I have never known an eel to take a fly.

Using the waterworks pool called for certain geographic deception. I'd have to start in the opposite direction and come back so nobody could see me. I'd come home the same way. One man who knew we were well trouted at my house used to sneak around trying to find where I really fished. I used to lead him to Asa True's Brook, which was a pasture-warm brook with nothing in it but chubs, and I'd fish away to make him think this was the place. I felt like a cloak and dagger decoy. Then I'd move around a bend in the brook and take off. He fished True's Brook all summer.

In time quite a few of us were poaching the waterworks, but mostly I had it for myself. I'd find out where the superintendent was fishing, and I'd keep out of his sight. But there were never too many, and the place never got fished out. I imagine when the water company was required to clean up and improve the flowage the plankton count fell off, and trout found the going a little tougher. But I was grown up by then.

We had other brooks. I knew where the spring-holes were on Goddard's Pond on Mill Stream. You could fish that pond and catch chubs, eels, hornpout, perch, pickerel, sunfish and bass until the cows came home, and swear there wasn't a trout in there. But in the springholes, even in hot weather, there were beautiful trout. And, we could turn seaward for fish. We still had some smacks that fished off Nova Scotia, and a salt fish factory, and there was never anything about salt-water fishing that we considered sporty. When the pollack were running any lobsterman was glad to have a bunch of boys go out with him to handline bait, and we always got to jig for mackerel. Mackerel will strike an unbaited hook, and we'd bring in a barrel of them. We'd all eat mackerel, and some of the women would put them up in jars, and then the season would change and we wouldn't see any more mackerel for a year. Some of the lobster-men would wash up their boats on a Saturday and take out Sunday parties to handline for cod and haddock. These boats would come in along in the afternoon with everybody burned red from the sun, and they'd have tubs of cod and haddock, pollack, and sometimes a halibut. Everybody in the party would want one or two fish to take home, and then the rest was up for grabs. I used to wonder why a man on a deep-sea fishing trip would keep on piling up fish after he had all he wanted.

Perhaps it was because it was a lot like trout fishing, and perhaps it was because the cunner is a sweet little morsel — of the salt-water angling I liked cunnering the best. The cunner is a sea perch, and although he gets fairish-large the ones we'd catch off the rocks were six and eight inches. The cunner is spiny and must be skun, but a pailful of them will produce one of the nicest fish chowders of all. But I never thought any salt-water fishing could beat the calm quiet of a secluded trout pool, and no fish ever pleases me so much as a trout when he favors me with his attention. No other fish is as pretty, either, as our Maine brookie. So I had paid my twenty-five cents for a license, and planned to get my value back. I certainly did.

THE RICH PAUPER

TODAY our Great Society frowns on distinctive terminology, but in my time we called half-wits half-wits. Today Willie Parker would be called indigent and retarded, and great effort and funds would be spent to rehabilitate him into a useful citizen and bring him social success. We were more honest. Willie had been shortchanged on brains, and we didn't believe this could be remedied by legislative act, however phrased, or reformed by welfare specialists and the laying on of hands. He was never in an institution, and he finally died a natural death in his own bed, with general grief. "Oh, that's a blessing — but whatever shall we do without Willie!"

Willie was a big, blubbery man of at least fifty, with the mind of a small child, which is kindly. He was harmless. The town supported him all the way, and had him in a little house up over the hill on the fringe of the village. As a recipient of "poor money" he became a bookkeeping oddity that afterwards drove the state auditors wild, and I suppose he was the only town pauper ever to die wealthy. He had a good life, but I'm inclined to think if he were living today the government policies would abuse him.

You see, in those days a town rather much ran itself. There wasn't this prodding down from state and federal levels to keep things stirred up and dependent, and if the local selectmen could keep the local voters happy things ran along very well. The voters decided every March how much they wanted to spend for each account, and the selectmen were expected to spend less if they could. To cover unforeseen items the town always voted two hundred dollars for the "contingent fund," and over the years this had become a handy thing. Our homespun bookkeepers, who were the selectmen, couldn't always decide what to do with some random item, so they'd throw it into contingency. One year they took the two hundred dollars, did forty-eight thousand dollars worth of business with it, and had seven hundred and eighty dollars left over. When the statehouse first began meddling in local government they sent an auditor down to check our town books, and he went eight feet in the air when he saw our contingent account. He said we couldn't do that, but we'd been doing it for a long time.

Historically, the year that first state auditor came was the year town affairs began to decline. Taxes began to go up, the annual printed report became deceptive and a whole flock of new notions flew over. Books that nobody can understand please state auditors. After that we weren't always so sure we understood town affairs, which until then was the one thing we did understand.

Willie Parker was handled under the "poor out." The elderly paupers, and those who needed bedside care, were put on the town farm, which nowadays connotes something it never did when we had them. It was a kindly place, comfortable and adequate, not unlike today's nursing home. Most of the snide objection to it was generated by social uplifters who wanted to get a whack at the relief money themselves. Our town farm often produced potatoes and cordwood until the account showed a profit, but since the time of the New Deal nobody has made any money caring for the poor. Those living at the Town Farm were the "poor in." Willie was poor out. Besides a roof, a visit now and then from Dr. Gilchrist, and occasional new clothes, Willie got a grocery order from the selectmen every week and picked up his own groceries at the stores. The storekeepers had an understanding with the town officials, and paupers were never allowed any frivolous things. Just the necessities. Willie would walk to the village and showed no dejected spirit at being the recipient of public alms. Indeed, his robust appearance was proof that he was well cared for, and it was good to see him around.

Willie always tipped his hat to the ladies. He'd take it away off, bow and say, "Good morning!" If he saw a woman up ahead on the street, going away from him, he would run past her, turn, and wait until she approached. When he tipped his hat she'd always say, "Good morning, Willie, thank you." Many a time we boys were told we'd do well to learn some manners from Willie.

One day Willie showed up for his groceries with a pushcart. He'd found some small buggy wheels somewhere, and had fashioned a body on them, with a leg to make it stand, and it had a handle. Willie was as proud as could be. Everybody admired it, and Steve Mitchell gave him a can of blue paint. Willie slapped it on, and his blue pushcart was a beauty. He would set it down on its little leg to tip his hat to the ladies, and they would say, "Thank you, Willie — my, what a handsome cart!"

So when Willie was in the town office the next time to get his grocery order Elmer Porter, who was selectman as well as lumber dealer, said, "Willie, why don't you empty the wastebaskets into your cart and go to the dump?" He did, and when he came back Mr. Porter gave him five cents out of his own pocket, and after that Willie was in the trash business. He'd go to the dump for anybody, and he always exacted five cents, and when he died years afterwards they found a nail keg of nickels in his house — he never had anything to spend them for.

The trash business led quite naturally to the swill business. In those days garbage was called swill, and as most people still kept some hens and many still kept a pig it had a home-front value. But the days were changing, and amongst Willie's trash there was getting to be more and more swill. Somebody complained that the dump was beginning to stink, and that rats were congregating, so Mr. Porter told Willie not to throw any more swill on the dump. This led to the pig.

They bought Willie a pig. They couldn't spend any poor-out money on a pig, so they dipped into the contingent fund, and for five dollars they got him a shote just the right size. This wasn't done in secrecy — everybody knew about it, and thought it was a wonderful idea. Now the ladies would say thank you, admire the cart, and inquire after the pig. Willie would spit all over his chin and recite the details. He went to the sawmill and cadged some slabs to make a pigpen, carefully separated the swill from the trash, and took a nickel for going to the dump but hauled garbage for nothing. We had a complete sanitation department in town and didn't know it, long before our time.

The next time Dr. Gilchrist was up that way he stopped to give Willie the usual town-paid health checkup, and he came barging into the town office and said Willie was all right but the pig was in trouble. The pig was standing hip-deep in swill and couldn't eat it as fast as Willie brought it home. The situation was nauseating and a public menace. Mr. Porter nodded, and bought Willie a second pig. Today a problem like this would be handled otherwise. They'd notify a board, engage an engineer, send out an inspector, conduct a survey, get a court order, close down the project, put Willie in a rehabilitation center, and raise the tax rate five mills on the dollar. But all Mr. Porter did was get Willie another pig. He got some more slabs, collected some more swill, and from time to time they got him some more pigs.

After a time Willie's first pig got up to about two-seventy-five, and Mr. Porter called Whitcher the Butcher. Locally this gentleman was known as Wootcher the Bitcher, for no particular reason. He conducted some services for the pig, and sold him to a man who peddled meat in the tenement section of Portland, which was far enough away to be safe. There was, of course, a tidy profit, and Mr. Porter entered it in the contingent fund.

This made sense at the time, but soon Willie's pig business exceeded a contingency, and Mr. Porter began crediting some to poor-out, and turning to the contingent fund only to pay back the cost of new pigs. But when Willie's income exceeded his current grocery demands, and poor-out was growing faster than they could spend it, they went to Judge Larrabee and asked how all this might be done in a legal and orderly fashion. What they did was set up a trust fund, with Judge Larrabee as trustee, and for his nominal fee he would handle the money. He'd turn grocery money over to the town, and buy new pigs, and then get the profits from Wootcher the Bitcher and build the fund up again. It finally got up to several thousand dollars, and there was no need any longer to keep Willie on the poor-out list.

But they did, for sentimental reasons, and he remained a pauper all the days of his life. The selectmen felt it was no disgrace to be rich.

When he fell ill he was provided with a trained nurse, and his trust fund paid for the funeral, including ten dollars for a lot in the cemetery. There was some debate over settling his affairs, because Maine law makes no provision for probating the estates of paupers. Judge Larrabee found some solution, and what Willie left went into the town welfare accounts, one way or another. This included the keg of nickels. That was the same year the state auditor first came around, and he asked a great many questions but he didn't seem to believe anything anybody told him. Because of the state auditor the thing was allowed to become hazy and indistinct, and it's pretty hard today to go back into the old records and find just where Willie was.

That's true of so many things.

THE SIDEWISE CAP

Mother believed round garters cut off the circulation and caused varicose veins, so she kept me in a pantywaist several years longer than most boys. Nobody knew this except me and Mother, and I was particularly careful to keep it a secret because there was a touch of ladiness to a waist after a boy got about so big. One of the biggest fights we ever had in the school yard was over a waist, between Duddy Blethen and Roscoe Melborg. Duddy accidentally revealed his underclothing during some recess activity and Roscoe began needling him about wearing a waist. The fight started, and they pounded each other up, and finally Duddy knocked Roscoe down and jerked up his shirt to reveal that Roscoe, too, was wearing a waist.

We all wore them, with varying times for giving them up. They were a vestlike thing with buttons around the bottom, and it would catch up your pants as well as the long garters to your stockings. I feel sorry for boys who get shoved into long pants as soon as they can walk, because they have nothing but socks to hang up at Christmas. My long, black, coarse-ribbed stockings came up over my knees, and on Christmas they'd hold about a peck. If activities were kept decorous, nobody needed to know you wore a waist. It didn't show unless you let it, and a boy coming up to about the time of his first long pants didn't let it. The waist engendered hilarity if exposed. One day I stood up in school to answer a difficult geography question, and as I sat down my garters got into some trouble, and there was an unmerciful snap of elastic and I was assaulted painfully in an intimate place. It jolted me about a foot in the air, and my whole body went vacant. Tears ran down my cheeks, and the teacher came to ask if I was feeling well. Nothing, of course, would make me reveal that I was still wearing a boy's waist with long garters, and since I couldn't otherwise explain my pain I insisted bravely that I was all right. It was the turning point; I never again wore a waist.

But I didn't get into long pants right away. We went into long pants when we approached manhood, and it wasn't at all childish to see boys wearing short pants who needed a shave. I'm not talking about knickerbockers, and the "plus four" style that was to come later. These were good, useful woolen pants that hung below the knee and buckled there. The buckle was almost tight enough to keep the long stockings in place, but if we didn't have a waist and garters we wore a circle of black fabric elastic, or a plain rubber band. The very best of these pants were of corduroy, and because the ridges swished when we walked we called them whistle-britches. All such pants went where we did, and if a pair that frequented a barn got wet in the snow and then dried off in a warm schoolroom the flavor was rich. Since corduroy was long-lasting, but got stiff if you washed it, pants of this material went on and on until their patina and sheen made them champions. Stewart Wainright had a pair that used to stink beautifully.

We had no dalliance with odd and casual clothing. It was long years after my time that the first old-maid schoolma'am raised a cry about girls in slacks and boys in sweatshirts. In our time every boy wore a shirt and necktie every day, and if we sported sweaters they were for warmth and not for looks. Most of us had a jacket, which we called a suit-coat. And it seldom matched the pattern of our pants. Shirts had detachable collars requiring brass collar buttons, and by using a fresh collar every morning or every second morning we could get good mileage from a shirt. This was good, because washing machines were yet to become endemic, and ironing was done with "heaters" off the top of the stove.

I never owned more than two neckties at a time, and these were of staid, dignified patterns selected by maiden aunts as Christmas presents. I would wear one day in and day out until it crumbled and fell apart, and then I would wear the other one. By that time it was Christmas again. Going to school without a tie was unheard of. Once I got a patent tie that came cemented into a perpetual knot, and it had a little hook that gripped my front collar button. There was no loop around my neck at all. I would just hang it on, and go. It had a decorous and subdued weave, such as a minister would wear at a double funeral, and all the boys admired it. It was the only one in town. After a few weeks the wire hook lost its reliability, and from time to time the thing would drop off and I'd lose it. Then a teacher or somebody would come bringing it to me, and they would make up fanciful tales about where they found it. The girl's basement was a favorite gag. I got so I was most careful to check my necktie before leaving any place where indelicacy might be presumed.

We showed great individuality in our caps. A hat, as such, was seldom worn — not only by us, but by any male in town. Except for church and going away. The cloth cap with a cardboard-lined visor and a snap might be of the same pattern as our jacket, but seldom was. We bought these caps at Bean's, and wore them until the cardboard in the visor was soft, pliable, dephlogisticated and the thing would hang down over our eyes like a damp pancake. In winter we wore stocking caps, and sometimes a leather cap with lambskin earflaps that tied aloft on less frigid days. But whatever we wore for a cap, it was tossing material. Drew Gilman once wrote a book of poems he called *I Throw My Cap on Sidewise*, but the day had passed and the critics didn't understand. Throwing a cap on or off was a talent, and when a boy came to school he flipped towards the hook, and when he came out of school he flipped into the air and poked his head under it when it came down. "Straighten your cap!" mothers used to say when we went out, but once out of sight you could adjust to suit. A real achievement in cap-throwing was to hit the hook in school without even looking to see if you did. Around the corner, flip! and right to your seat. Stewart Wainright mastered the nonchalance, but he never mastered the flip. Two or three mornings a week the teacher would say, "Stewart, go and hang up your cap!"

On our feet we wore boots most of the time. As distinguished from shoes. Lion Brand was a favorite, and if we kept the neatsfoot and tallow on them they'd last a long time. The rubber-bottomed hi-cut was about to appear, but we could still get cowhide tall boots that came up over our calves. The Lion Brand boot was, of course, ankle-height. In summer we went barefoot, or wore moccasins or sneakers. Moccasins were better then than now — they were made of heavy belting leather, now hard to find, and they didn't have soles. The sneakers would come apart if they got wet. Today you can toss sneakers in a washing machine, but if we walked in the dew with them they would give up. Unwashed, they gained a ripe consistency, and smelled like somebody locked in a small room smoking Turkish cigarettes. Mothers didn't like sneakers much, because they thought they made our feet sweat. They did.

In winter we fought a constant conflict between heat and cold. We walked to school no matter what the weather, and we would sit all day in the heat, to walk home afterwards no matter what the weather. There were no thermostatic controls, no ventilation features, and the teachers had no authority over the janitor. One suit of long-legged drawers probably outweighs a whole roomful of today's underwear. Some cold mornings we'd arrive at school to find our ink frozen, and in an hour or two the room would be so hot we'd have to open the windows, and then the ink would freeze again. One girl in our class, even then a holdover from antique notions, wore a bag of camphor on a string around her neck to ward off colds. She had a cold as often as any of us, but she made the school smell like a moth-proof closet. Some days we'd sit in our shirtsleeves and sweat, and through the windows see the sky turn leaden and the first wisps of snow come against the panes — before school-out we'd have a good foot of snow, and drifting. We'd haul on our sweaters and jerkins, mackinaws and stocking caps, and walk home — ignorant that a day would come when schools would let out early for storms so the buses might get around. And that if the snowplow didn't get around soon enough in the morning to give the buses bare roads, there wouldn't be classes.

One February, just before the Washington's Birthday vacation, we had a ripping storm that struck soon after school opening in the morning. "I can tell you when the snow will begin," said our teacher, who was one of the good ones. "Do any of you know how I can tell?" Today the world is full of high-priced meteorologists who can't tell, but our teacher could, and she did. She passed the *Old Farmer's Almanac* to Michael Stevens and said, "Michael, do you know how to look up the tides?" So she showed us all how to look up the time of the high tide, and when Michael found the next one was at 10:42 A.M. she had him go down front and write 10:42 on the blackboard. "I suppose you all know what A.M. means?" she said.

Of course about 10:42 we saw snowflakes at the windows, and we all chirped up. "A northeast storm usually shuts in on the high or low water slack," our teacher said. "It's a pretty good weather rule. You watch it, and you'll see that it seldom fails." I've watched it ever since, and it's a pretty good weather rule. That afternoon the outdoors was a wild, driving maelstrom of biting snow. Our legs were shorter then, and it was hip-deep to most of us. We were dismissed at the usual time, and with caps close-hauled we started for home. When we came to the end of our street I was on ahead, followed by six Pendletons, four Rodways, Annie Gilchrist, my sister, two Lawries, Bobby Conway and Charlie Hawes. Charlie dropped off at his house and the rest of us kept on. Indian file we came along up the hill, and my sister and I turned off to leave the others still going. My mother had set the broom in the shed, so we swept each other off and went into the kitchen. Mother said, "How come you didn't bring any books home tonight?"

It snowed all night, and it was still snowing hard the next morning. My sister and I got ready, and when we saw the Pendletons, Rodways, &c. wallowing down the hill we went out and fell in ahead of them. When we got to school and had our heavy clothes off, our teacher began the day by saying, "Now you'll find that a northeast storm usually clears off the same way it begins, so does anybody know how to figure today's tide from yesterday's?"

Another thing about our clothing and the way we dressed: our pants had watch pockets. The wrist-watch was unknown, but we had a much finer timepiece — the dollar watch. You could pay more for an Ingersoll watch, but the one that cost only a dollar was the easiest to come by. They were a good watch, but the local jeweler charged two dollars to repair one. So if your dollar watch ceased to function you fiddled with it yourself, sometimes successfully, and if it wouldn't tick again you tossed it away. The watch pocket, now largely gone from men's suitings, was a starboard bow repository you could locate by the fob hanging down. The fob was of leather or cloth. Inside the pocket one end attached to the watch, and then the rest would hang down in front to give you a handle if you wanted to know the time. It was difficult to reach into the pocket with thumb and forefinger and bring out an unfobbed watch. There was a little gesture of finesse to whipping out a watch by the fob. Some boys, unequal to a whole dollar for a watch, would just have a fob, making believe there was something on the end of it. If we found out a boy was faking this way we'd plague him by asking him what time it was. The answer to us was, of course, "Just about." Or, "Quarter to." Nobody fooled anybody very much.

The finest way to dispose of a spent dollar watch was to let a train run over it. Somebody would announce to general enthusiasm that his Ingersoll had kicked the bucket, and we would all go down to the railroad with him to see it run over. Freight trains were best, and the late afternoon down-freight would have the then-legal hundred cars. Loaded with potatoes and rolls of newsprint they'd be pretty heavy. When we saw the train far up the track, just hitting the downgrade through our town, the watch would be laid on the rail and we'd all go back and sit where we could see it. Those old freights rousted right through — they had steam, momentum, and an engineer with a good arm for pulling whistle cords. I suppose as he looked ahead from his cab he'd see us sitting there, and perhaps guessed what we were about. Suddenly four hundred wheels with the force of a thousand triphammers would pound that watch, and after the train had passed we would rush over to see what beauty had been wrought. The Ingersoll watch would be tissue-paper thin, ironed out to about a foot long, and we could see every gear and wheel and spring flattened together and welded into a perpetual pattern of Time. I had one hanging on the wall of my attic room, forever pounded into an unalterable half-past four — so thin I could hold it against my kerosene lamp and see light through it, and well worth a dollar right there. And after I flattened my Ingersoll I wore my fob with a difference until I could scrape up the price of another, and when somebody asked me the time I would say "Just about."

THE RESPECTED CITIZEN

O NE morning in the fifth grade Lawrence Maxey raised his hand and told the teacher he had a stomachache, so she helped him into his boots and coat and he went home. We never saw Larry alive again, and it was our first brush with the grim reaper. At the hospital doctors said he hadn't been brought soon enough, and the next day we sat in school and couldn't keep our eyes off that vacant seat. We had found that seats may become suddenly vacant. Miss Dunham told us we should all bring twenty-five cents for flowers, and go to the funeral together.

I can see that wreath in the church as clearly now as I did then. It was made from "pinks" because we didn't call them carnations then, and they were pink and white. The long satin ribbon said, *Classmate*. The fussy background of brakes and asparagus fern was the unvarying touch of Perez Burr our florist, and Mr. Fish our undertaker had thoughtfully arranged the "piece" in the spot of honor at the head of the casket.

We walked together from the schoolhouse with Miss Dunham to the fore, and we were more bewildered than sad, baffled than shocked. Mr. Fish had saved two pews for us directly behind the family, and in his best tippy-toed manner (I looked to see if he was wearing sneakers) he ushered us efficiently, with the air of sharing deeply our great grief. He left us to fidget in the awful stillness that precedes a church funeral. After the services Mr. Fish returned to whisper that his classmates might now pass forward to pay their last respects to Lawrence, and we had not expected this.

Somehow I didn't know, nor did my classmates, that Larry would be "exposed" — a word I later found is good mortuary parlance. I thought, from anything I could see from the pew, that the cover was shut. Each of us in turn was astonished when we passed by and found Larry there. Except for Charlie Munsey, who had "lost" his grandmother, none of us had ever gazed before on the still face of death. Miss Dunham capably stood by and laid a reassuring hand on each shoulder as it came along, and we were thankful. Then Miss Dunham led us back to the schoolhouse and read us a story to shift our attention. She let us out early. The next day we found all the seats had been rearranged so we had no vacant one to stare at, and the little tags on the cloakroom hooks had been moved up.

After that, intact, our class went along. We never lost another. Sometimes I hear talk of the barbarities of former times, and it may be so — and we

164

must have been a healthy lot. If you look in the town records of those days you will find that most people died of "Old Age." We had any number of folks in their eighties and nineties, and they would come to the end of their book and die of old age. Today the records tell of coronary occlusions and contributing causes. But Dr. Gilchrist thought old age was cause enough, and if he went into details he would say "seizure" or "stroke." One certificate says, "Cause of death: A fall." That was Malden Hooper, and the fall was about eighty-five feet. That was the closest we ever came to a murder in all the years of my growing up. His family did call it murder, but the man who pushed him denied it.

Well, Malden was one of these people who gets a couple of drinks aboard and wants to fight. A bunch of men were having a quiet clambake, with some spiritous assistance, and Malden announced that he would take on anybody two falls out of three. After a time somebody pushed Malden and he fell off the cliff. After they finished eating the clams they went down to see if he had been hurt, but he was dead so they decided it hadn't hurt him very much.

Whenever a "respected citizen" died the stores would close for the funeral. And not just pull the front blind and use the time to restock the shelves; the storekeepers would go to the funeral. You'd see the meatman take off his wristers and straw hat, part his hair before donning his coat, and join the other merchants on the sidewalk to walk in a group to the church. Some of the chain stores today don't even

165

draw their blinds. We didn't have funeral parlors then, and if a man served as pallbearer he actually picked up the coffin and carried it. Malden Hooper was a respected citizen, and the stores all closed for him.

There was but one suicide in town in my youth. I can't remember if he hung himself or blew out his brains, but it bothered me for some time. They said he was "despondent," and it was pretty hard at my age then to figure out what that meant. I'd sit and look off and wonder about it. It must have been pretty important.

And we didn't have any accidental deaths, either. Once in a while somebody would fall off a staging or get stepped on by a horse. A finger might get left under a clicking machine at the shop, or somebody would kick at a belt in the sawmill. But these things didn't kill anybody. Even our early automobile accidents were hardly fatal — many times they didn't even hurt the automobiles. It wasn't until the grade-crossing accident came to be daily fare that we could see the motorist was a menace. For a decade or so the railroads thought they owned everything, and they thought blowing a whistle took the curse off doing eighty over a blind crossing. We had one crossing where the gate-tender went home at six, and the fast express came along at six-ten, and they'd pick somebody off about every night. But that was later. I remember one man who got struck by lightning in his lobster boat, but probably that wouldn't be called an accident. It blew his shoes off, and while the men carried him up over the banking to the road I walked along behind bringing his shoes. At the time it seemed like the thing to do with them. But mostly we went living right along, and that's what we thought the days were for.

THE RACEHORSE

OUR house, where my attic room was topmost, had as much mystery as history. The house looked as if it belonged right there, but people told us the front part had been drawn on in two pieces by oxen, and used to sit on the other side of town. The ell was added from reclaimed lumber, and afterwards they built our barn. The whole thing ran together after the Maine fashion. This explains why we had a back stairway that didn't go anywhere, and how in afteryears my father found a part of the cellar he didn't know about.

And he didn't know about the barn chamber until after he'd bought the place and moved in. Barn chambers were catch-alls for family accumulations, and were wonderful for rainy-day play. Old trunks were full of clothes. There were piles of books and magazines, and old letters. Nobody ever slept in the barn chamber except boys on summer nights — it was like going camping but you didn't go anywhere. But our barn chamber, when my father finally went up to look at it, was very different — ours was a poker palace and dope mill.

The previous owner had fixed himself a hideaway. Two couch hammocks were suspended from the rafters, facing each other, with an oak poker table between. Ash trays, chips and cards were at the ready. Dad snapped on the green-shaded lamp overhead, and it cast a bright light downward so you could easily tell jacks from queens, but it didn't glare up the barn windows to alarm the neighbors. Then over on the other side of the chamber was a long bench lined with jugs, gallon cans, medicine bottles and several great kettles. A dozen or so pasteboard boxes were stacked up, each holding a dozen six-ounce medicine bottles that bore the label Win-A-Race. The label said the product contained ninety per cent alcohol, and was harmless to animals if used as directed.

This whole thing was as illegal as murder. It was never difficult to get racehorse dope around the fairgrounds, but the place of origin was always a secret. My father now knew that his barn chamber had been the place, and he quickly rearranged everything before anybody could find out about it and accuse him. He put the two couch hammocks on our front porch, my mother kept begonias on the poker table, and the cartons of Win-A-Race were hidden behind beams in the dark corner of the chamber's carpentry. By the time I was old enough to remember, our barn chamber was just like any other barn chamber —

full of old window blinds and screens with holes in them, broken chairs and replaced bedsteads.

Horse trotting, more properly called light-harness racing, had not in those days been tagged by the state tax collector for support of the blind and elderly. Parimutuel betting was still far from enactment. Betting on anything was illegal and dishonest. Most of the horses that raced were locally owned—they didn't pad the cards by fetching in out-of-state professionals. Many farmers and horse fanciers raced their own nags, or had somebody like Whisperin' Gleason to do it for them. The betting was vest to vest, and probably far more honest, man to man, than it is now under state supervision. And if in the exuberance of a friendly tilt you put up too much money on your own horse, you might try to gain a few seconds through a dose of Win-A-Race just before the start.

I found the bottles stashed over the beams, where my father had put them, one rainy day and sniffed at one of them. A horse doped with the stuff would have smelled like a New Year's drunk, and the back row in the grandstand could have winded him from the backstretch. I could see how it might pep a horse up, but I wondered what took place if all the horses had Win-A-Race. The sniff from the bottle confirmed in me my father's original suspicion — that a group would gather in the barn chamber to manufacture as much Win-A-Race as they thought the next meet would require, and then they would drink what alcohol was left and play cards.

It was years after that, late in August, that I answered a knock at the back door and found Whisperin' Gleason standing there. He asked in a crashing confidential crescendo if my father was home, and from the front room Dad thought the cow had come into the kitchen to blat. Whisperin' said his business was confidential, so my father nodded for me to scoot, and I went out by the woodpile where I could hear everything. Whisperin' Gleason never said anything privately. "Was wondering," he said, "if they's any Win-A-Race left around? I got Raffles entered at Gorham, and they's one horse I mistrust. I think some Win-A-Race would solve everything."

This was the first time we ever knew that anybody had knowledge of our barn chamber and its illicit business. My father protested that he didn't know what Gleason was talking about, and kept telling him to keep his voice down. Dad vilified all who would dope a horse, and Gleason wheedled. I got the idea, though, that my father was being bugged by his own curiosity, and I wasn't surprised when he went up in the barn chamber to look and see if, by any chance, there was just one odd bottle left lying around. Whisperin' tried to pay him for it, but my father wouldn't take his money.

We were pleased to hear that Raffles won at Gorham. But Raffles also won at Fryeburg and Windsor, without needing any Win-A-Race. Then Whisperin' Gleason came back. "Farmington looks bad," he bellowed. "Horse from Bridgton could beat Raffles. I'd like another bottle."

My father would be the last person in the world

to dope a racehorse, or abuse any animal. But he was bemused about the efficacy of his inherited product, and he had this Whisperin' Gleason hollering on his doorstep. The best way to get rid of Gleason was to give him some Win-A-Race, and the best way to study the effect was to see how Raffles made out. Raffles won at Farmington.

It was the night before the free-for-all at Topsham Fair that Gleason came back. The free-for-all at Topsham was the last big race of the season, and owners who had been holding their horses back all summer to keep from "marking" them could let go in this event. Next year the marking would start all over again. Raffles would surely need his all. Whisperin' Gleason made the details public on our back porch, and my father stood there in the noise and said no. "Go on, get out!" he kept saying. He told Gleason just what he thought, and it wasn't much, of any low-down, scoundrel, scalawag of a rotten skunk that would feed dope to a racehorse. "If I weren't mixed up in it I'd turn you in!" my father yelled back.

Whisperin' Gleason was aghast. His feelings were hurt. "Good Gawd, Frank," he said. "I never give none of that stuff to Raffles! I drink it!"

Evidently my father had no compunctions about doping Whisperin' Gleason, because he gave him a bottle. Topsham Fair was the only one we went to. Schools kept Columbus Day, and they gave us the middle day of the fair off, so the whole town went to Topsham Fair. My father led me by the hand through the crowds, past the cattle sheds to the horse stables. The drivers were getting ready for the free-for-all, and we found Whisperin' Gleason leading Raffles around. Raffles was steady and keen, but Whisperin' Gleason was stumbling over some things that weren't there. Gleason was glad to see us, and let me pat Raffles on his soft nose. Raffles didn't smell one bit like the bottles in our barn chamber, but Whisperin' Gleason did.

My father cleaned house then, and poured all the remaining Win-A-Race down the sink, and that was the end of that. Raffles won the Topsham free-for-all in a breeze. Had no trouble at all. He was retired after that, if you call being at stud retirement, and our barn chamber retired with him. Whisperin' Gleason never came back. We figured he found another bootlegger.

THE BIG GIANT

I N the day when a wind-up train with eight lengths
of track was the most sophisticated toy on the
market, and not many around, a real motion picture
projector was beyond credence. Frank Small had a
motion picture projector all his very own, and until I
got my Big Giant steam engine with the whistle he
rode a high wave of distinction. I played a small part
in getting him the projector.

Well, we didn't have toys, much. Sleds and carts,
and later bicycles, but Christmas was mostly for
mittens and sweaters and good, sensible presents. I

used to get a lot of books because you could buy a book then for twenty-five cents. We didn't ski then. If we had skis they were the brown ash kind made here in Maine, and they had a strap over the instep. We always slid down a track. If some bumbling booby fell down and spoiled the track we'd wait at the top of the hill until he fixed it. We had tobog- gans and bobsleds, though, and unsanded hills to ride on. There was no dearth of things to do — I don't mean that; but we didn't have too much in the way of smart toys.

So when Frank said he was going to sell a Larkin order and get a movie projector I thought that was wonderful. Larkin was a sort of precursor of Avon and Stanley, and a cake of Larkin soap was consid- ered the ultimate in high-toned ablutions. A boy could "send in" for a Larkin order and win wonder- ful prizes. According to the catalog this projector was a handsome thing. It would throw clear images across a room, and was suitable for large gatherings. It could be used for church and lodge entertainments. It came with a reel of pictures all ready to run. After Frank sent in for his Larkin order we would sit and look at the catalog and lay plans for picture shows — we might even put the Nordica Theatre out of busi- ness.

The big stumble with the order they sent Frank was the picture postcards. Besides the usual soaps and salves, there came a thumping great wad of highly colored view cards showing Niagara Falls, the Grand Canyon, and swan boats in the Public Garden

— exotic delights of small local interest. We walked our legs off trying to foist these cards on our little community, and the only way we could sell any was to say this was all we had left and we'd get our projector as soon as we sold them. We wheedled the "last lot" away a dozen times, and everybody knew about the projector and was much interested in it. The last cards were badly rim-wracked before we suckered them off. Frank sent in the money, and then we waited and waited. It got so Frank would start into the post office and the clerk would shake his head through the window. People who had bought dog-eared picture postcards and thus felt involved would ask if the machine had come, and some suggested perhaps Larkin had gone out of business. But one day it came, and Frank had to sign for it at the post office. We ran to his house with it and opened the bundle.

It was certainly a beautiful thing. Complete and ready to go. Well, almost ready. We had to do something about illumination. Today you just plug something in and switch it on. But we didn't have very many plug-in receptacles wired up then, and this wasn't an electric machine anyway. The instructions told us how to fill, adjust and operate the carbide lamp.

This was no great problem. Carbide was the basis of the acetylene gas lamps common on bicycles and the older motorcars. Some homes and stores used it. We even used carbide for Fourth of July fun, and knew how to blow a tin can over the treetops with it.

The principle was simple — water dripped on the chemical and created a gas that would burn with a very bright white light. So bright it would project pictures on a screen. We ran to the drugstore, got some carbide, ran back, and soon heard the little hiss coming from the jet. We touched it off, and there was the projector all ready to project!

The screen was a sheet Frank's mother helped us hang up, and on it we saw the wonderful action of the "reel" that came with the machine. This reel turned out to be a loop of celluloid perhaps three feet long, joined on itself so it went round and round and round through the projector and repeated. There were no spools, no rewind. And there was a hand crank. Frank turned the crank.

It was a Fatty Arbuckle picture. Fatty Arbuckle was an oversized human who made comedy out of his proportions. He was the pie-throwingest of them all. In those days he was the best the motion picture industry had found for the one-reelers of the five-cent days. (The World War Victory Tax hiked the nickel to six cents.) A funny picture with Fatty Arbuckle was tops. Now Frank had a Fatty Arbuckle picture show all his own. In the three feet of looped film Fatty climbed a stepladder and fell off, and by that time the cycle had gone around so he would climb the ladder again and fall off again. After Frank got tired cranking I did it awhile, and there was a sameness to everything. We cranked until the carbide was exhausted and the flame died out, and by that time the projector was so hot we couldn't touch it for an hour. The black enamel burned off the thing, and the room smelled like a hot stovepipe. Nobody ever found any other pictures to run through Frank's projector, but if you cared to see Fatty Arbuckle falling off a stepladder it was just the thing. Somehow we never felt Frank had been cheated. It was a motion picture projector, and that's what he wanted.

I made out much better with the free premium I won from Perry Mason. Thanks to Erle Stanley Gardner the name Perry Mason now means a lawyer-detective in California who never loses a case, but it was not always so. Erle Stanley Gardner was born in Malden, Massachusetts, just outside of Boston where, in his boyhood and in mine, the Perry Mason Company published the *Youth's Companion*. It was a fine magazine, published the big-name writers of the day, and added classics to literature with every issue. Its circulation was immense, both foreign and domestic. With quiet Boston dignity it finally died of the same disease that killed the *Transcript*, and at about the same time. Like Larkin, Perry Mason had prizes to reward juvenile efforts, and the finest prize they ever offered was the Big Giant steam engine — a "real steam engine for young engineers." Not a locomotive on a track, but a stationary power plant of great beauty. The Big Giant was made specially for Perry Mason, and could be acquired only by finding a new subscriber for the *Youth's Companion*. Plus postage and thirty-five cents for handling. I can only wish to today's boys the magnificent yearning that I had for a Big Giant. Toys that come easy are too cheap. It was hard to get a Big Giant.

The reason was that everybody took the *Youth's Companion* anyway, and finding a new subscriber was worse than peddling Larkin picture cards. Besides, even if you found one, you still had to have thirty-five cents and the postage. "Check with your postmaster," the come-on in the magazine said, "and he will instruct you on how much postage to send." I checked, and it was eight cents. That meant I had to save up forty-three cents. But I got the forty-three cents, and I got a new subscriber, and I sent in for the Big Giant. Like the projector, it took centuries upon dawdling centuries to arrive.

It, too, was a beautiful thing. It did stand eleven inches high, and it did have a polished brass boiler, large balance wheel and a whistle. It could be run for ten hours at top speed steadily at a cost of less than one cent. It would run a buzz saw, and as soon as I made one with a cardboard blade it did. And since it never blew up on me I assume it really was "free from danger of explosion." It had one flaw — a minor one. It burned kerosene for fuel, and it made more soot than the evening freight on the uphill grade to Deep Cut. My mother discovered this when she came into the living room, and she kicked me and the Big Giant out. Then my father discovered it when he came into the barn, and he kicked us out. For years I would take my Big Giant out onto an elm stump behind the buildings and play with it there — billows of black smoke rolling down across the fields until the neighbors thought I was rendering pogies. But I was a young engineer.

I have no idea what became of my Big Giant, but so much of youth passes the same way. She whirled her balance wheel for years, and I played with it long after I should have outgrown such frivolity. It was never a Fatty Arbuckle thing, even though the flywheel went round and round the same way. It was faithful and true, always fun, and then one day I just didn't have it any more, and it was gone. I haven't the faintest. Perry Mason, in the *Youth's Companion,* said this Big Giant was valued at $2.75. I would guess the item went off their lists along about 1922 or 1923, but mine was long gone by that time. I would gladly pay ten times that for a Big Giant now, and I would play with it. It was the best toy I ever had.

THE TWO AUTHORS

THERE wasn't too much culture in our town, and it is amazing that I was exposed to two real live authors there. If they left an impression on me I shan't be surprised. I can't say what brought these two amongst us, but they were there and I knew them both well. Otherwise, theatricals were home talent; concerts would be piano recitals by the reluctant pupils of Bess Bennett; art was hardly more than hooked rugs at a Mizpah Class summer sale. The beckoning world of belles lettres fought uphill through the picky committee that bought a box of new books once a year for the Carnegie Library — they read everything first to see if it was fit for the rest of us to read. They held back on reference works because we already had the complete *Stoddard Lectures*. But in that climate we had two authors.

Aubrey Ruggles was a milkman and had a place out on the Pleasant Hill road, about two miles from town. He was a newcomer, but was making out. He waited until he got the feel of the community before he pitched in. Very smart man. Then one year he arose in town meeting and delivered a remarkable speech. We were accustomed to homespun, pithy remarks by farmers and storekeepers, but Ciceronian eloquence in measured classic form was something else again. Mr. Ruggles was exposed as a gentleman and a scholar. A deep hush lay upon the citizenry, and they rallied to whatever it was he espoused. Then the next year the Republicans ran him for the school commitee. Usually it was easy to defeat a newcomer, and the Democrats should have had some luck that year, but such was Mr. Ruggles's unlikely esteem that he sailed into office and proved to be "a good man for the schools." Unlike other school board members, he used to come and visit classes. No matter what we were reading he knew how to ask us questions about it, and he generated a lot of enthusiasm. We liked to see him come walking in. So the next time we had a speaking contest I asked Mr. Ruggles if he would coach me.

I would stick the book in my hip pocket and walk out to his place, and after he got the milk strained and in the cooler he'd hear me recite. Mrs. Ruggles was a sweet, quiet lady who folded her hands in her lap like Whistler's mother and listened without betraying either interest or disinterest. They had a coocoo clock on the wall, not a little one such as tourists bring home, but a real baister that boomed. It would always coocoo while I was there, but the session never lasted a full hour and I would be gone before it coooked again. Mr. Ruggles let me know that he had done some playacting in his time, to explain why he wanted me to say certain words a certain way. He would stop me and say, "That's a good word, don't slur it — give it all its juice!" And one evening he showed me a magazine that had just come and it had a story in it by Arnold Reeves. "I wrote that," he said.

I could see how this made sense. A for Aubrey and Arnold; R for Ruggles and Reeves. I gave the words their juice and asked him why Arnold Reeves was better than Aubrey Ruggles. He laughed and said he guessed it wasn't, but he liked to be anonymous. I read the story and I thought it was clever. He made grist of "etc."

"I love you, etc.," said the hero.

"Kiss me, etc.," said the heroine.

"I shall return tomorrow for the money, etc.," said the villain. "The house is on fire, etc.," said the sheriff.

There were about three hundred etc.'s in the story. Then Mr. Ruggles heard my piece, offered some suggestions, and I ran home to spread the word that we had an author in town. Nobody would believe me. Authors are rich, and why would a rich author be wasting his time peddling milk? Still, there was that speech he made in town meeting, and he was fine on the school board — perhaps he was an author! After a while people believed he was an author. Nobody but me ever saw anything he wrote, and that was by Arnold Reeves.

Our other author was Ferdinand Berthoud. He arrived in town one day and took a room at Dennison's where he spent a precise time every day whacking at a typewriter so dishes jingled in the china closet. Unlike Ruggles, he had ample proof of his production. Around the walls of his room, on the floor, he had stacks of pulp magazines, each carrying one of his stories. On the wall he had two charts. One was his plot formula and told him in which chapter he did this, in which he did that. They were all boy-meets-girl things, and the locale was always Africa. He said he grew up in Africa. In one story somebody would get shot in chapter three, and in the next story he would get stabbed in chapter three. Then drowned, burned, trod by elephants, and so on. But whatever it was, it happened in chapter three. The other chart was a graph showing his wordage for the day.

Maine was new to Berthoud and unlike dark Africa, but he fell in love with the place and took long walks by himself. On one of these walks he discovered Noble's Camps down at Flying Point, and thought this would be a splendid place to retreat during the long winter and concentrate on his chef d'oeuvre. He would come out in the spring triumphant. Noble's Camps were not what we call winterized. In the camp Berthoud selected the vast stone fireplace at one end was designed to tickle the fancy of summer complaints during the heat of July and August, and was not meant to warm anything up. The camp was on cedar posts and had single flooring.

The roof was flintcote paper. Not too much of this showed up during the pleasant weather of September and October, but when November froze around the edges Mr. Berthoud took notice. He found he was spending more and more time each day chopping wood, at the expense of his masterpiece. He detected new and errant drafts every hour on the hour, and he brought in a big canvas tent and pitched it before the fireplace, with the flaps right against the stones. This cut off some drafts, but not all, and caught up some of the heat, but not much, and whenever he came out of the tent he had to take the side down. He was in bad shape not only from cold but from poor eating when somebody happened to think of him along in January. Vic Coffin, who lived at the fork of the road just above, waded down through the snow and called in for a toboggan and ambulance. As they loaded Mr. Berthoud on a stretcher he stated that he found more heat in cutting Maine wood than in burning it. The author of a thousand desperate struggles in jungle and desert found a Maine winter instructive. He spent a time in the hospital and was all right. We almost lost him, but he rallied.

The next summer we really did lose him. He packed up, said good-bye to everybody, and moved away. That next Christmas some of us had cards from him, and he said he was all right, was living comfortably in a Washington Square apartment and was working for the *New York Times*. We got the idea he was quite happy and prosperous, and we understood the *Times* was a very good paper — but we didn't know anybody in New York so we never took it.

Other than that I was never exposed to literary figures in my youth.

THE OTHER VERSION

S TILL, you can't always be sure what is literary. It
was years after growing up that I found Mark
Twain's story about Cap'n Josiah Mitchell, and real-
ized I had been exposed to it long before. I'm sorry
Mark Twain couldn't have conferred with me before
he wrote it, because I like our version better and I
could have given him some hints. Particularly about
the harelip. Cap'n Mitchell had a harelip, or some
similar speech defect, and when folks in my town
told of his great deeds they always imitated him by
talking through their noses. Mark Twain interviewed

Cap'n Mitchell and wrote him up — but he never mentioned this. Yet the *Honolulu Advertiser* said Mark Twain's story was "a clean scoop of unusual magnitude and an admirable piece of literary art."

You'll find the story, re-polished for magazine use, in Mark Twain's collected works with the title "My Début as a Literary Person." So we assume this is the story that, of all others, Mark Twain believed launched him on his career. By stretching the thing a mite we can say, perhaps, that my town created Mark Twain, because my town sent Cap'n Mitchell to sea.

It is one of the grandest tales in all the annals of sailing. Cap'n Mitchell's vessel was the *Hornet,* a holdover clipper of extreme design, hailing from my town and already holding records of 113 and 107 days, New York to San Francisco, when in 1866 she left Pier 11 in the East River to see if she could negotiate the passage through the Straits in even faster time. She never completed this voyage. My town and Mark Twain differ in some of the details. The way we heard it a seaman heard something dripping in the dark hold of the *Hornet* off the coast of Chile and struck an old Portland Star match to see what it was. It was kerosene, so Cap'n Mitchell, with his crew and passengers, was adrift in the longboats on the broad bosom of the Pacific watching the *Hornet* burn up on the horizon.

Two of the *Hornet*'s boats were never seen again, but the one with Cap'n Mitchell and fifteen others began a forty-three-day trek across the ocean to the nearest reasonable land — the Sandwich Isles. This is our fiftieth state of Hawaii, but to boys growing up in my town they were the Sandwich Isles. The trip was, and you can get the details from Mark Twain, a grisly experience. If you recall the story of Lieutenant Bligh in *Mutiny on the Bounty,* you will thrill to find that Cap'n Mitchell beat him in every respect — more people, smaller boat, fewer supplies, longer course and greater elapsed time, and that Mitchell encountered worse weather and heat. They ate their boots, and even chewed fat from the staves of a butter tub. But they stayed alive, all, and they came ashore the morning after they'd eaten their last food the night before. Kanakas welcomed them and fed them back to health. They recovered at beautiful Hilo. And Mark Twain, then thirty-one and ill, was vacationing at Honolulu, interviewed Cap'n Mitchell and produced his story — first called "Forty-three Days in an Open Boat.'"

But Cap'n Josiah Mitchell was left forever, in Mark Twain, on the Beach at Waikiki, and this could not be true. No Maine story could end there, and Cap'n Mitchell didn't stay there. Anybody from my town cast up in the far places is going to come home, and that's what Cap'n Mitchell did. Penniless, his seafaring fortune gone with the *Hornet,* he went to the waterfront to see who might be around. In those days Maine skippers could say howdy-do to folks from home in any port in the world, and it didn't take long to find a Maine vessel that had a place for him. He hitched a ride, working his way, and came to Melbourne. From Melbourne he hitched to Calcutta, then to Rangoon. And such was the way they traded then that he sailed the greatest of great circles, coming always nearer home but doing it the long way round. He got to Shanghai, and caught a vessel to Valparaiso. Around the Horn then, and up to Liverpool. Down to Marseilles, and across to Norfolk. From Norfolk he caught a coaster to New York, and another to Boston. A sloop carried him to Newburyport, and from Newburyport he walked home to Maine. He had spent four long years coming from Honolulu home!

He arrived in our little village footsore and weary just at suppertime on a warm August evening, with the birds singing in the trees along Main Street, and because it was suppertime nobody was out to see him come. Four years earlier he had left here, going out past Punkin Nub and Pound o' Tea, dipping his flag to the harbormaster's farewell salute and flipping the customary "shillin'" into the tide — buying fair winds and a safe return. The shilling was a good Yankee quarter, of course, and the mud flats there must hold a barrel of good-luck coins — quite a few from Cap'n Mitchell in his time. Now he was home, and he walked through the village and came at last to the clamshell walk to his own back door. He turned in, and he stood a brief moment with hand outstretched — about to lift the latch on his own portal.

Cap'n Michell's Penelope was named Kate. Kate, like mariners' wives all down the long seafaring years, had occupied herself in Jose's absence with patient waiting, and had found some solace in religion. That evening she had prepared her frugal meal and had eaten it by the breeze in the back kitchen window, and after doing up the dishes had hurried into her church clothes so she could attend evangelical prayer services that were being held that week in a tent across the way. A revivalist, a young fellow fresh out of a Bible school, was bringing his whoop-it-up gospel to the hinterland, and he had touched Kate with his inspirational message of Hope and Faith. It is not good for Woman to live alone, either, and in four years Kate found she needed constant bolstering for her stoicism. Each evening that she had gone to the meeting she came home spiritually revived. Now, ready to go again, she depressed the latch on her back kitchen door, still pulling on one glove, and found her husband standing there about to come in.

None of this is found in Mark Twain. What does a man say to his wife after four years of absence? What does a wife say to her husband after four years of praying for his return? Face to face, a mere threshold apart, what do you do?

Kate, with the prayer meeting in the tent on her mind, perhaps did a rational and sequential thing. She was the first to respond, and she said, "Oh, Jose — you've been spared to me! Come, we'll go to church together and thank our God for this happiness!"

Certainly not Mark Twain, and least of all our

local tellers of tales, gives us a hint of what Cap'n Mitchell said, or thought. He must have been weary unto dropping, and his mind must have been confused, because he went — and Kate marched him down front to the seat nearest the pulpit. She certainly wanted everybody to see that he was home. And then the worship service began — the invocation, the anthem, the message from the Scriptures and the offering. The long prayer and the impassioned sermon. Then they came to that part where all are expected in turn to rise and testify, in their own words and from their own emotions, about the goodness of the Lord.

This one did, and that one did. The Lord was kind to many, and they were glad to say so. And as the interest flagged the young minister saw Cap'n Josiah Mitchell sitting there, and having no inkling of who he was or whence he came, he thought to draw him into the fellowship and make him feel wanted. He leaned over the pulpit, stretched his arms toward Cap'n Jose, and warmly he said to him, "And now won't you, sir, rise and tell us what the Lord has done for you?"

Let us remember that Cap'n Mitchell did have a split lip, and that public speaking was not his best talent. Let us recall, too, that he was just home from a long and unpleasant experience, and that he was not in church through any considered intent, and that he had not planned to testify.

He didn't stir. And the minister besought him again. And now dear Kate nudged her husband and smiled to bring him confidence. This was, of course, a literary moment, but I never knew it until years later when I read Mark Twain.

Cap'n Jose stood up. He looked about the tent, seeing many faces he had longed to look upon during the past four years. He turned to face the minister, and in the same booming voice, so nasal, that he could use on the deck of his vessel and be heard in the mastheads during a no'theast blow, he told what the Lord had done for him.

He bellowed, "He damn-nigh ruin-t me!"

THE DUPED MICAH

T HERE had been a fairgrounds and horse trotting
park in my town, and I suppose that offers a
background with certain tendencies. It is sad to see
old places of amusement fall apart — horse sheds
rotting into the ground and grass growing on the
racetrack. The big exhibition hall had been turned
to the street and made into a two-family house, but
everything else was left to time and desuetude. The
half-mile track where for so many years the horses
raced was one of the best in Maine. The hard-packed
clay and gravel surface didn't get too muddy in foul
weather, and the bog it encircled held moisture so it
never dried out too much. But all this was in the
past. The "trotting park" was already legendary in
my time.

The bog grew excellent cranberries and I used to
gather enough there for Thanksgiving sauce. If I
got them just before the first frost they were juicy
and tender, and big as glass alleys. And after the

first frost, when fall rains had swelled the bog over the bushes and weeds, the trotting park was the best skating in town. We could go to the old horse sheds and rip off boards and timbers for our big bonfires. And for the first two-three snowstorms we'd shovel and broom the snow back and keep the ice clear. No municipal appropriations, no recreation supervisor — we did this ourselves because we wanted a place to skate.

In truth, the place was public. After the fair association failed up, the property ceded to the town, so here it was available to our uses, and all ours. Nobody saw any future use for the area, beyond a skating pond, until my uncle the iceman reflected that the hay growing on the racetrack would be wonderful insulation for packing ice. He offered the selectmen three dollars for the stumpage, and they seemed to think this was a fair price and couldn't see why not, so my uncle cut the grass.

There were some quips about mowing at a 2:10½ clip, and if a pacer raked as well as a trotter. The hay was full of thistles, burdocks, hardhack and mullein and wasn't good for anything except to pack ice, and it wasn't a howling success even for that. But it was the smoothest haymaking anybody ever tackled. The mowing machine ran on and on without a hitch, for there were no rocks, ditches, candle knolls and old surprises to fetch up on. I raked the track for my uncle, and made believe I was in the free-for-all. The judges' stand was long gone, but I imagined one and I could feel the eyes of the race officials peering down on me as I brought in the winner. Twice around was a mile. My uncle hauled the hay down and piled it near the icehouse for future reference. You'd think that might be the end of the story.

But we had another sterling character in our town who had an amazing propensity for bumping his head against my uncle. He was a cow-buying, horse-trader, semi-veterinarian and random entrepreneur of anything that came along. He had a fine reputation as a sharpie except when he locked horns with my uncle, and just that summer my uncle had bested in some kind of a horse deal that rankled Micah. Micah Dwelley was his name, a big, robust, pompous fellow about five feet tall. Like all shorties he had to strut a little to make his pace show, and somebody had observed that Micah was able to strut sitting down. He was able to look bigger than he ever was. With my uncle, I guess Micah larded his dickers with some personal animosity, because there was talk that my uncle sometimes consoled Micah's wife whenever Micah went away now and then to take the Keeley Cure. This may have been only the surmise that went with being the iceman, or it may have been so. Anyway, Micah was currently looking for some way to get even, and he grabbed onto the trotting-park hay. A town, he argued, had no right to go into the hay business, and the selectmen not only shouldn't have sold the trotting-park grass to my uncle, but they should have asked a good deal more money for it. Three dollars was ridiculous. Suit should be started, he claimed, to recover the full value of the hay, and to punish my uncle for civil trespass. Nobody took Micah seriously, but he generated a lot of talk, and my uncle gave the situation some thought.

He mused on it quite a bit. Then he went to the selectmen and said he guessed they had made a big mistake; that Micah was absolutely right. He said he could see how a constitutional issue was involved, and that a municipality could not lawfully profit from the sale of hay on tax-ceded land. Very clear to him, he said. It was a technicality, but a proper one, and Micah for once was in the right. My uncle had just happened to bring Secretary Potter along with him when he made these remarks, so the *tête-à-tête* would not remain *sub rosa,* and Secretary Potter was eager not to miss a word.

My uncle concluded that the only fair solution he could think of was to return the hay to the town, and for him to get his three dollars back. At this he winked to the selectmen, but Secretary Potter was behind him and didn't see the wink. When Secretary Potter trotted to Micah Dwelley and reported all this, Micah was upset. This wasn't just the way he had planned things. He therefore hastened to the town office to protest, saying the hay had been sold, and the town had no use for it, and the only proper way out was to make my uncle pay a fair and decent price, which he seemed to think ought to be as much as eighty dollars. The selectmen said they would give some thought to his remarks, and then went and asked my uncle what he thought they better do.

My uncle then said that Micah's contention left

them with only one way out — he would have to buy the land to legalize everything, and if they would pre-date a deed he would give them five dollars for the trotting park, or two dollars more than he had already paid them, and this would have to satisfy Micah. They did, and he did, and Secretary Potter brought the glad news to Micah, who was sad about it.

After that the snows came, my uncle packed his ice with the hay, Washington had another birthday, and the springtime returned to our town. Indeed, June appeared on schedule, and the meadows waved with daisies. Two strange men appeared in town then, and began asking questions. Their purpose was veiled, but they inquired about tax rates, availability of factory hands, rental housing, and suchlike things. They went to the grocery stores and asked if people in our town were slow pay. The impression they conveyed was that they were the forerunners for a large and wealthy corporation which was considering our town for a factory location. They were, however, the icemen from two towns at the other end of the state, and the impression they gave was wholly erroneous. They did, after working up excitement all over town, arrive at Harry Dunbar's livery stable, where they held a long public conference, in private, with Whisperin' Gleason. Somehow Whisperin' was able to glean from things they let slip that they were selecting the site for a big plant to manufacture automobiles, and that the trotting park was the only place that would do. Perceiving that they had carelessly revealed more than they intended they swore Whisperin' to secrecy, which he readily promised.

As soon as Whisperin' told all this to Secretary Potter, Potter ran to Micah Dwelley with it, and Micah said it was very interesting. He asked Potter if he thought my uncle was aware of these guarded inquiries, and Potter said, "Don't think so; nobody knows 'cept Gleason and he just tumbled to it from something they didn't mean to say."

So Micah Dwelley happened, right after that, to saunter into my uncle's little office to inquire about a colt he heard might go on the market, and after preliminary sallies he chanced to mention the trotting park and wondered if my uncle still owned it.

"Sure do," my uncle said. "You gave me a goosing on that deal. Pretty clever the way you worked it. But no hard feelings. I been thinking about it, and I have half a mind to fix the old track up and use it for training. Charge a small fee by the season, and maybe get some of my money back."

"You only give five dollars for it," said Micah.

"Eyah, but it still was an ungodly sticking. But I don't mind. Bygones is bygones. Would you train a horse there if I was to fix it up?"

"Might. Depends on what you charge. You wouldn't be interested in having me take the trotting park off your hands, would you?"

"Oh, no," said my uncle.

"Cost a lot to put that track back in shape."

"Yes, but it'd be kind of fun. Ain't too many

people in this world ever get to own their own race-track."

"I don't suppose they's anything else anybody could use the place for."

"God, no," said my uncle. "Sure isn't."

"I'd buy it if the price was right," said Micah.

"You're talking foolish," said my uncle. "Why, right now I wouldn't take a thousand dollars for the place."

"I'll take it," said Micah.

So my uncle sold him the trotting park for a thousand dollars, and Micah sat around waiting for the two men to come back about the automobile factory. They never did come back. Micah paid taxes on the trotting park for a few years and then let the town have it again by default. The hay on the race-track was never cut but that once. Years afterwards the state highway commission ran the new interstate route that way, and if you drive past my town today you'll whiz right over the place of our old trotting track and never know it. Nearby is a sign that says animals, ridden, driven and led, must be kept off the roadway, and all farm implements over ninety-six inches wide. It's the new rule. But I drove a horse in a horse-rake right there, twice around to the mile. There were no rules then about many things.

THE BIG ROCKET

T HE firemen in our town did have one good rule — nobody could have a fire without giving ten minutes' notice. For a volunteer department this was about what was needed and time and again I saw houses burn down when, if the hose had come ten minutes sooner, they might have been saved. The department was assembled by ringing the bell in the steeple of the hose-house, the steeple being not only a belfry but a place to suspend the lengths of hose so they'd drain dry. By my time we had gasoline-driven fire-pumpers, but the old handtubs were kept for fun at musters. Once a year, on the night before the Fourth of July, our firemen didn't sit around home waiting for the bell to ring, but reported in force around twilight to be ready. Firecrackers and rockets could ignite dry shingles, and sometimes did. So the firemen would stand around on the alert.

In our square stood a three-story building with

rents. Three stores occupied the ground floor, and
Judge Larrabee had his office on the second — otherwise the space was given over to small apartments.
On the rear of this building a heavy vertical wooden
ladder had been spiked, not only as a fire escape for
people living in the building, but as access to the
roof. It ran right up by the third floor. The roof
was flat, of tar and pebbles.

One night before the Fourth I was standing on
the sidewalk across the street from this building,
helping Ruel Hanscom watch for fires. Ruel perhaps
didn't know I was helping, and I had no professional
status. Probably I had run out of firecrackers. Just
standing around. Ruel had two pails of water at his
feet and thus far nothing had occurred to put any
strain on them. If anything should happen, other
firemen with other buckets were stationed within
earshot. Now, as we stood there an intense and enter-
taining drama unfolded before us, involving this
three-story block across the street.

Young Widgery Toothaker lived on the third floor
in one of the rents, with his father and mother, and
he was amusing himself this evening by dropping
lighted firecrackers on people down on the sidewalk.
The store front directly below Widge was that of
Artie Mitchell, who handled the town's fireworks, and
consequently quite a few people were milling about
waiting for anything that might perchance. Ruel and
I could see Widge's head pop out, the firecracker
descend with its trail of fuse sparks in the night, and
then we would hear the report and see somebody on

the sidewalk go ten feet in the air. The lucky recipient of this explosion would then accuse the fellow next to him of dirty pool, and denials would flow. Widgery would wait a decent interval and then drop another. Ruel and I watched this, and Ruel chuckled to himself about it and allowed the boy had a good thing going. Nobody on the sidewalk knew where the attack was coming from for quite some time — but Widgery was finally discovered up there and retribution set in.

First Ruel and I saw two heads pop out over the end of the flat roof, right over Widgery's window, and then pop back again out of sight. "Something's doing up there!" said Ruel. Shortly the two heads appeared again, and now Ruel and I could see the sputtering fuse of a lighted salute come down, and it dangled on a string exactly in front of the face of Widgery Toothaker, who leaned on his elbows at the sill and stared at it entranced. You could see that he had not expected this. I heard Ruel say, "Duck! You fool, you!"

Widgery did not duck, but when the salute went off it bounced him back so he must have fetched up against the far wall, and by that time I had left Ruel and gone around behind the block to start up the long wooden ladder to the roof and see for myself just who had engineered this tremendously successful event. I took each rung of the ladder carefully in the dark, and went up with moderate speed.

Well, a few minutes before young Widgery was blasted thus, his father had wakened from his bed, and as he roused up it seemed to him he heard footsteps on the roof above. Knowing that fire could occur, he wondered if something might be amiss, so to find out he stepped through his bedroom window onto this same ladder, and ascended until his head was above the roof and he could look out over the tar and pebbles. He did of course see two boys over by the street edge, and at that moment he heard a blam as his son was blown up, and just then I came up the ladder and climbed between his legs up inside his long nightshirt.

I have never decided which was the worse — to go up inside as I did, or to have somebody come up inside as he did. There were a rough few moments, during which Mr. Toothaker articulated exactly what he thought of the idea, and it wasn't in favor. I managed to hang on in spite of the flailing he did with his bare feet, and came down to run back and stand beside Ruel. Ruel said, "He was asking for it." Every few minutes Ruel would mention it again. "Damn fool sat there and stared at it like he was mesmerose!" Mr. Toothaker never knew who blew up his boy or who invaded his privacy — but he offered five dollars reward if anybody would tell him who did the former. The latter he never mentioned, and neither did I.

Another exciting night before the Fourth was the time Asa Mumford set off the nine-dollar skyrocket. When Artie Mitchell displayed his fireworks that year he brought up this monstrous rocket and stood it in the window. The tube of the thing was about three feet long, and we'd never seen anything like it. We could get skyrockets for ten cents then, and we were tremendously impressed when Artie said this huge one was priced at nine dollars. So many inquired the price that Artie finally made a little sign to put on it, to stop the questions. Since few of us had more than fifty cents for our little bag of snapcrackers, and by good management we could make that last through the holiday, Artie's chances of selling a nine-dollar skyrocket were slim. Quite a few parents, picking up things to shoot off on the lawn, made Artie offers of three and four dollars or so, but he stuck to nine dollars and said he wouldn't take a cent less. The handsome thing was still in the window, although most of the fireworks had been sold, and it was already ten o'clock and getting late. Then Asa Mumford showed up. Asa had been to Portland, and he got off the ten o'clock trolley to see if there might be some way he could make the evening notable. He was tanked like a milk depot, but not with milk, and for some reason was wearing a buffalo-skin overcoat. He hadn't been off the car ten seconds when somebody dumped a lighted salute in one of the pockets of this coat, which blew the coat apart and filled the night air with buffalo hair. This pleased Asa, as it proved he was one of the crowd, and because it was a large salute and expensive. He spied the big skyrocket standing in Artie Mitchell's window and said, "Jee-rooslem!" He marched in and tried to dicker, but Artie still hung out for nine dollars. So Asa came out of the store and began passing the hat. "Come on, come on," he said. "Put your money where it'll be heard from! Cough up, and we'll shoot off the big rocket!" I put in my nickel, which was all I had. Asa went around behind the buildings and put the bite on all the firemen, and he had to go around twice before he had nine dollars. I was particular to notice that while everybody cheerfully responded to Asa's ideas, he was not amongst those who dropped coins in his hat. He dumped the hatful of money on Artie's counter and came out with the beautiful rocket.

Somebody brought a drain-trough from a downspout to make a chute for the rocket, and somebody else brought boxes to prop it up. Some of the firemen aimed the chute, hoping to drop the spent embers in a field somewhere, but some of them said they thought the thing was big enough to go right out to sea. Artie Mitchell had said the thing was supposed to blow a whistle, give off a shower, cast out bombs, and finally release a red flare that came down by parachute with an American flag. Asa said, "Well, for what we're paying it ought to do something!" Asa propped the skyrocket in the chute, and we all formed a circle at a respectful distance around the square. We were going to see the nine-dollar rocket after all!

Asa also withdrew a discreet distance and lit a new cigar. He had a little trouble bringing the match against the end of the cigar, but he finally got it puffing and announced that he was quite ready. He walked out, reached at the fuse of the rocket with his hot cigar, and I never heard any bigger stillness than we had at that moment. It lasted quite a while, because Asa was also having trouble finding the end of the fuse, and we had to stay quiet while he hunted. Then he backed up and said, "I don't think it's any good — I can't get 'er to light!"

Somebody said, "Stay with it — she'll light!" Asa went back. And we all went to being quiet again. When the fuse did catch there was no question about it. A spurt of bluish flame shot down past the end of Asa's cigar, and he jumped back about twenty feet. Unfortunately, as he jumped back he jolted the fuse somehow, and he tipped the skyrocket backwards out of the chute so it lay there sputtering on the ground, rolling a little. Nobody knew what to do, so there was a great popular wave of doing nothing. Asa helped a great deal by shouting, "Run for your lives!" but nobody moved an inch. We stood there fascinated, staring at the huge skyrocket with its spitting fuse the way Widgery Toothaker had stared at his salute — each of us in an ideal situation to be spitted on nine dollars' worth of fire with an American flag. Which way would the thing go?

When it went, with a mighty burst of thrust-powder, it caught the lip of the trolley car track and turned right up Main Street. It went with a whoosh for about two hundred yards, and then climbed about two feet in the air and stayed at that altitude. It missed everybody, and that included Sourpuss Harry Bundage, who was the janitor at the Baptist Church and had been hanging around to see that the boys didn't ring his bell that night. He was standing out in the street looking up and down, and this rocket went by him as he stood there. Nobody ever found out where the thing came to rest, but it must have been in a far place because we looked all summer for an American flag on a parachute and couldn't find it. But in the town square that night we were all thankful it went somewhere without skewering anybody. Asa said, "Never saw the thing — I hid behind my hands, and when I come out it was gone. Never saw it at all!" But Ruel Hanscom said, "I saw it. And I never see nobody spend nine dollars so fahst!"

THE LAST REUNION

THE big difference with holidays then was that we didn't have anything else to do and spent our time observing them. I don't believe Abraham Lincoln knew that the ice goes out of our Maine lakes in time for Memorial Day fishing. I can remember precisely when Memorial Day ceased to be Memorial Day — it was the year the American Legion took over the conduct of the exercises and told the Grand Army veterans that things were in good hands. The Grand Army of the Republic had dwindled, and the few old comrades still left were unable to march behind the band to the cemetery. So the new veterans put the old boys in the back seat of an automobile, rushed the program through, and a new day had dawned. After that the occasion was a quick run-through of prayers and bugles, and a chance to get home fast and go fishing. For one thing, with new efficiency the Legion boys started putting out the flags and geraniums on the Sunday before, so they'd have that much done and needn't take time on the holiday.

We had five Grand Army men left when this change came. They called each other comrade, a word that has become dirty since their time. They had shared more than the campaign hardships of the witless battles in '61 to '65. They had become elders together in a small town that loved and respected them, and each year they had shared the reunions of Memorial Day. There was bound to come one year when the last old soldier still survived, and with us he was Otis Coffin. Still spry and bright, he attained that greatest sorrow of life — to be alive when all others are gone. At his last regimental reunion he was the only man there — nobody came to speak to him, and he sat alone in a chair for an hour or so and then went home.

Our later wars have not given us veterans like those old soldiers. For one thing, the wars are different. But it was the times, and the mellowing of years when other people had time to care. There was dignity to being a G.A.R., and the men themselves never allowed you to forget it. Right up to the last,

Otis Coffin used to walk the mile from his home at the Landing to the stores and do his shopping with a string bag. He spoke to everybody, everybody spoke to him. He gossiped about affairs, and would walk home — satisfied the community would fare all right until he could return tomorrow to help again. In town meeting he always explained the plans for the Decoration Day exercises, and the citizens voted him the requested hundred dollars to buy flags and geraniums and hire the band. On Decoration Day he took charge, and made the choice of a speaker.

This wasn't hard. Anybody holding public office was expected to turn out on Memorial Day and give an oration somewhere, and with us it was usually a Hale. Maine had a Hale in public affairs right through our history, up to the time Bobby Hale fomented a Democrat majority, and in my time it was Senator Frederick Hale. He always gave the same speech every year, and he always concluded by repeating "Thou too sail on, O Ship of State, Sail on, O Union, strong and great!" Most Maine people thought Freddie Hale wrote it just for Memorial Day, and I was surprised myself when I found it, later, in my Longfellow book at school.

Otis would get the line of march straightened out on Memorial Day morning, and the band would step off with a brisk pace toward Maplelawn Cemetery. As they reached the gate they would shift to a dirge and step to one side, so the old soldiers marched in past them to take places by the graves. Each soldier was carrying small flags and pots of geraniums and petunias, and there was every evidence that intense personal grief welled in his heart as he took his position. A prayer was heard, the band played again, and on command from Otis the soldiers stooped to set the flags and fit the flower pots into the little recesses by the headstones. Then a bugler sounded taps, to be answered by another bugler down over the knoll in the distance, and the band quick-stepped the veterans back to the gate. It was customary for the band to play "The Battle Hymn of the Republic" as it came forth from the graveyard, and they played it with a cadence and tempo not heard today from any orchestra, band or choir. The Republic, I think, may have been a mite nearer to us then.

At the stone statue of the Boy in Blue, between the two park cannon, Secretary Potter had drawn on a hayrack hung with bunting, and this was the platform for the address. Somebody always repeated the Gettysburg Address, and then Senator Hale would beatify everything good and vilify everything bad, and tell the Ship of State to sail on. After the exercises the old fellows would sit around, and stand around, and wait for noon when the Women's Relief Corps served the baked bean dinner in the K.P. Hall. It cost twenty-five cents, but the old soldiers were not asked to pay. There came that year when Otis was the last-left of all the knights, and visited around after he had his pie, and patted us boys on our heads, and finally started to walk home with the remark, "Good-bye — see you all next year!"

For Otis there was to be no next year.

Nor the Relief Corps. We never had another Memorial Day baked bean dinner.

Otis had been the commanding officer at the attack on Vicksburg. We found everything about the campaign against Vicksburg in our history books except that Otis was in charge. How the first part of the year was spent in engineering an attack, and along by July everything was ready. On the third of July the sappers were ready, and General Grant set the big assault for the sixth. But on the third of July General Pemberton of the Rebel defense met with General Grant under a tree and agreed to unconditional surrender. On the Glorious Fourth the Union flag flew over the Vicksburg scene. Otis said all that was true. He was an orderly for a captain in Grant's command, and during this period he was in a position to know. Then on the fifth of July an order came for his captain to turn out and arrange the details of parole and surrender — each soldier had to sign that he wouldn't fight again, each cavalry man was to take a horse home with him, and so on. Otis was distraught. His captain had been off on a toot, and Otis had laid him away dead drunk on his cot in the tent, and there was no way to rouse him for this important duty. "I never seen nobody so stinking drunk as he was," Otis used to say. "It took more to sober him off than it took to take Vicksburg." So Otis pulled on the captain's uniform coat and borrowed his hat and went over and set up the surrender program. Everything went off fine, and after Otis got Vicksburg all taken he went back to the tent and poured cold water on the captain and got him back to his feet. Just then a courier from General Grant came with a citation for the captain, telling him what a wonderful job he had done taking care of the surrender, and saying he was going to suggest him for promotion. "That's the part that didn't get into the records, and you won't find a word about it in your books," Otis told us.

Otis was the first person in our town ever to act in the motion pictures. He went to the first meeting of the Maine Three Quarter Century Club, which Governor Ralph Brewster had thought up to show how people who live in Maine live longer than other people, and Otis was in the Pathé newsreels. It showed him playing checkers, and pitching horse-shoes, and running a bag race, and finally he was in the big Golden Wedding parade. Otis had been a widower for decades, but there he was on the screen at the Nordica Theatre with a good-looking woman on his arm! "We was both married fifty years, all right," he said. "But not to each other."

But the American Legion put Memorial Day on rubber tires and found out that one wreath laid on the cold marble of a centrally located cenotaph can symbolize all grief with one quick prayer. They also introduced the tossing of a wreath into the outgoing tide. By this time a fishing license had increased to a dollar and a quarter.

THE LONG COD

O NE lovely morning in school I raised my hand in history class and suggested that the Pilgrims must have been a stinking lot. I had arrived at this wonderful conclusion all by myself in a logical process of research and deduction, and I was a little proud of it. It seemed so vital to me that I was deeply hurt by my teacher's rebuff. She was certainly not one of my better teachers, and she operated on the approved theory that the Pilgrim Story should always be esteemed sweetly and presented in terms of piety and fortitude. To her, Elder Brewster could not possibly have worn underwear.

My deduction was, however, a simple thing. The Pilgrims left England in September, aboard a crowded and poorly equipped vessel, and they didn't arrive inside the crook of Cape Cod until late November. The history book said, ". . . all the women went on shore to wash, and so Monday has been kept as washday in New England ever since"* In these terms, it

* *The Beginner's American History* by D. H. Montgomery (Boston: Ginn and Company, 1902).

occurred to me that Provincetown was high time for soap. This was not, actually, a thing that popped into my head all at once, because I already knew that if perceptions are kept alert you can *smell* history.

Down on our tidal shores we had shellheaps. Professorial archeologists would come and dig in them and call them kitchen middens. They are the dumps of ancient people of five thousand years ago who came there to feast on the abundance of fish, and it was a lot of fun to go and dig in them. One of these shellheaps had been eroded by the ocean until you could dig straight into it horizontally, instead of going down. Five and six of us at a time used to take a lunch and spend bright summer days poking into these heaps to see what we could find. Once in a while we'd get a stone arrowhead or a piece of crude pottery. The best part of this outing was just being there — as if we were sharing the sea and the sky and the bright summer weather with other little forgotten boys of long, long ago. We would dig a mess of clams and cook them in a pail and throw shells over the bank — and wonder if some day somebody would come and dig in our shellheap to find out about us.

So one day I was digging into the banking, and I found a fireplace. It was smaller, but made just like the circles of rock we used to heat up to cook lobsters on for a Merchants' Picnic. The first stone I picked out was the size of a baseball, and then one by one I found the rest of them. I smoothed off a spot on the beach so I could turn around and reassemble the stones in proper position. The fireplace was about two feet across, and just a little concave. I found quite a few things in the ashes around the stones, and it was great excitement to lie there on my belly and study history. I found, of course, that I could smell the dead embers of a fire that had gone out five thousand years before I was born. I tried to tell another history teacher that in terms of our town Babylon was a recent event, but he wouldn't let me change the subject either. I tried to tell him the book didn't make me smell Nineveh, but he said that was quite enough.

Amongst the ashes of that fireplace I found the vertebrae of a codfish, each piece like a button. I laid them out on a board, tail to head, each button in sequence by size, and I found this fish was three feet long. This is a good cod, and even on our deep-sea fishing trips with strong handlines five miles outside we had never taken one that big. How would an Indian get him? Not my history teacher, but Humpy Dixon, told me part of the answer. "Big cod come inshore," he said. "Right time of year you'll find them in the creeks and surf. They didn't have to go outside to get big cod."

"How would they hook them?"

"Probably shot them with an arrer — might have spear-poked them."

And this was true. Charles Hawes was shotgunning down at Bunganuc one time and he heard something flailing around in the shallow water, and he shot a two-foot codfish with number six shot. Charlie brought it home thinking nobody would believe him, but it turned out that all the older folks knew that cod would come inside.

So that cleared up part of the mystery, and I found the rest of the answer right in the fireplace ashes. It was a beaver's tooth. Sometimes bog beavers get a little lazy and don't grind their teeth down as they ought, and the tooth will grow. This is the sharp chewing tooth of the lower jaw, and if it gets away from a beaver it will grow up around in a circle and come right into the top of his skull. If he hasn't died of starvation by that time the tooth will penetrate his brain and do him in. So the old Indians of five thousand years ago made use of this, and they'd find a beaver tooth that had grown out too far and make a fishhook from it. Probably lashed it to a long pole, and with a little bait on it they could jig a three-foot cod right ashore. I was cunner fishing one time, some years afterward, and through an incoming comber I saw just such a cod as that. He sucked my little winkle in and when I jerked he never knew anything about it. My little line parted, and he rode in on the comber and then drifted back out again, and as far as he ever knew he'd just eaten a winkle. I think if I'd had a beaver tooth on a maple pole I might have got him.

So the old shellheaps became a kind of history book, and in my mind I re-created those hordes of people who used to come to our town and throw their clamshells and fishbones over the bank. Of course there was a fire, and it made flames and gave off heat. It kept people warm, and cooked their food. Perhaps all this was squaw work, and the Old Indian I pictured never lifted a finger . . . The fire lighted the place at night, and shooed off the no-see-ums, and when a codfish was tossed on the hot rocks there was a sizzle and the delicious aroma of food. You can, if you imagine the right way, think of five-thousand-year-old codfish and find your saliva juicing up. I guess history books in school never make anybody really hungry. I used to picture this Old Indian, coming back from his trip up country to find a beaver tooth, and he walks out of the woods and looks around to see if his old friends are back, and he says, "Hello, Charles! Hello, Sarie! I'm back!" And then he'd say to his squaw, "Why don't we make camp right here by this tree?" I knew my tree wasn't there five thousand years ago, but he must have had a tree, too. And when I would tie one of my crude chicken-feather trout flies and show it to somebody I would say, "Just wait til I waft this over the pool!" Didn't the Old Indian show his new beaver tooth the same way, and the very next day on the incoming tide didn't he hook a three-footer?

I used to wonder about numbers. If all the people who have lived in my little town spent all their time gorging on seafood, it would take them ten thousand years to start a small shellheap. And we know that on the Long Trail, the old Indian route up the North Atlantic Coast, the original Interstate Ninety-Five, there are places where granite has been worn by passing feet. Not heavy hiking boots, but bare feet and soft doeskin moccasins by the hundreds of thousands, going and coming. There must have been more people lived in Maine five thousand years ago than live here now!

And so I came to wonder about Elder Brewster's underdrawers, and what they must have been like when he came to Provincetown. Monday has been a perpetual historical reminder in New England of the tattletale gray of the Pilgrim hegira — but we never seem to get any teachers who will admit that John Alden used soap. I think in their time an unwashed Pilgrim probably gave off an aroma of some kind. History, like a shellheap, should say so.

THE FORENSICS

Every time I won a prize in a speaking contest I would get an invitation to go to the next meeting of the Woman's Club and declaim the piece that won me the prize. This was a great honor. It was also my introduction to the Maine manner of getting a free program — today most of our knife-and-fork societies have an artistic scroll they give their honored guests so he can prove he spoke to them, and if the nasty question of an honorarium arises they will give you five dollars to help on gasoline. Yet I believe in public speaking as a required cultural pursuit — just as we used to pursue it in the old days.

Most boys and girls sweated through public speaking, and there was no great effort by teachers to bring them ease and confidence. The teachers could have done about what Dale Carnegie made a fortune doing, but they seldom took a stuttering Demosthenes aside and told him about pebbles. Pick something from the "speaker" — a book full of acceptable declamations — then memorize it and be ready when called. For platform-leery students this was torture. We could have been shown the beauty and grace of artfully constructed lyrics and addresses, the magic of bright words and the joy of pronouncing them. "That's good — I could hear every word!" a teacher once told Ned Coffin when he blatted out "The Dead Ship of Harpswell" as if he were yelling a voting list across the bay at a deaf ballot clerk.

I still think it was good for us. You can't walk through the woods without brushing the ferns, and some few of us did get the feel of poetry and the sense of spoken language. We got to know, more than anything, what it means to have the attention of an audience. What you say and how people react is the essence of all history, and you may be there to precipitate a revolution, or just to say What-is-so-rare-as-a-day-in-June. The only thing we were not permitted to foment in our public speaking efforts was humor. Humor, as a communicable commodity, was outlawed. One year I memorized that bit in Mark Twain where the American tourists ask the Italian guide if the mummy is dead. The place rocked and afterwards everybody told me I was wonderful, but the judges gave the prize to a girl who wept in iambic pentameter about unrequited love. Nothing in all the world is so joyful to a speaker as the sound of his audience in laughter, but we never studied this. Nothing in writing or acting is so hard as to make people laugh — they will cry at anything — but this technique was withheld from us. We bawled through speaking programs.

I finally fixed the Woman's Club. I forget if it was "A Message to Garcia" (which I pronounced gar-sha) or "The Man Without a Country" that I gave, but it was one or the other, and when the invitation came to entertain the Woman's Club I wondered why the members hadn't come to the contest if they wanted to hear it. So I appeared on schedule, scrapped my touching little declamation, and did a rousing job with something from Kipling which jingled, "A woman is only a woman, but a good cigar is a smoke!" I won several speaking contests after that, but was never asked to the Woman's Club again.

I was, however, asked to take a dramatic part in the Christmas pageant at the church. This was a vast community project that took shape one fall, and it was intended to put Christmas on a permanent basis. The general topic had been frittered around with some over the years, but nobody had ever yet nailed it down. This year everybody had a hammer. I borrowed Ike Skillin's commandery sword and played the part of that great general Judas Maccabaeus, who for some reason I can't explain arose and repeated the Twenty-third Psalm between Epiphany and the Death of Herod. I did not, you can see, have the stellar role.

This was played by a hundred-watt electric bulb inside a cardboard box, the box being on a traveling wire overhead, and having a cut-out, five-pointed pattern so it became the Star of the East. The wire turned around some bicycle wheels, the same kind of a rig they had in L. L. Bean's shooting gallery to carry the targets back and forth. The Star of the East would thus precede the Wise Men down the aisle as they appeared for the manifestation, singing "We Three Kings" as they came. When this scene came up the Magi took their positions, the song started, and somebody turned the crank on one of the bicycle wheels. The gearing hadn't been figured out correctly, and the Star of the East shot the length of the church, smashed into the front wall, the cardboard box crumpled, and the hundred-watt bulb dangled brightly as if it had something to do but couldn't remember what it was. They rewound the star and started again, this time allowing much better.

There was not, really, much hilarity over this, because we were in church at a presumably dignified occasion. But when the Wise Men arrived at the manger one of them who was our school superintendent hiked up his Chaldean bathrobe so he could kneel, and this revealed his long-handled red-flannel underwear. The seat of learning was exposed to the public gaze. This could not be passed unnoticed, and it wasn't. By the time I repeated the Twenty-third Psalm some of the bedlam had subsided, but now and then it would break out again.

Being a platform orator also got you into the casts of our wonderful three-act farces. There was a publishing house that made a business of printing play books, and you decided which one you wanted after you found out how many people you could get to be in the cast. If the senior class had seventeen scholars equal to dramatic performance they would pick out a play with seventeen parts. This was straight arithmetic, because seventeen players meant thirty-four parents to attend, as well as brothers and sisters and boyfriends and girlfriends. These plays were done by formula, and they used the hokum and corn. Almost all of them had a scene where double-talk threw the audience into hysterics. Two actors, for instance, would talk, and one of them thought he was discussing a boat, and the other thought he was considering a woman. "She's kind of rough on the bottom," one of them would say. Then he'd say, "Of course, two or three of her ribs are loose." Then he'd say, "She's kind of bulgy about the stern." Sometimes this ribald innuendo was too severe for a decorous community and our English teacher would rewrite the scene, but not always with success. We learned a lot. We learned how to ravel a rope and make moustaches. This would make an elderly bank president out of a high school boy. A poke bonnet would make a grandmother out of a vibrant young damsel full of adolescent vinegar. The hardest part of the play was the inevitable kissing scene when all injustice had been rectified and all impurities simmered down. For some reason these plays never matched up the boy and girl who were presently fooling around. No matter how careful the costuming and how infinite the rehearsals, the two young lovers always kissed cautiously. They were supposed to be Truehart Harry and Lady Van de Vere, but everybody knew it was really the Williams boy and the Martin girl, and they couldn't see each other for sour apples. Either one of them could kiss the ears off a fair adversary, but on the stage this night their sheerest ecstasy of unbridled passion looked like a diplomatic cessation of open warfare. They always looked like two children being forced to eat their oatmeal.

"Wielder of the stateliest measure," wrote Tennyson about Vergil — but did you ever stand on a platform and repeat an audience into a stupor with "The Courtship of Miles Standish"? I did that once, and have always believed Vergil, Tennyson and Longfellow needed, most of all, a good stiff course in public speaking.

THIS I am SURE is ex-ACT-ly what THEY should have HAD in their PRO-GRAMS.

THE COAL MAN

Sometimes men can be driven to crime by most plausible routes. This happened to my uncle. As the iceman he saw his prosperity melting away to the electric refrigerator. He was also the coal man, and he saw the fuel oil business liquidating him. He wanted something with security, so he became a bootlegger. As the ice and coal business fell off he mastered the art of getting a load of booze down the pike, and one day he was able to devote his full time to it. It worked out well. At the time I speak of I didn't know too much about rum-running, but I have a feeling I helped him one day. He had asked me to go for a ride with him.

He had a Hudson. A Hudson Super Six, which was guaranteed to do sixty miles an hour. I suppose it would have if we had had any roads you could drive sixty miles an hour on. If you got a Model T over thirty it would bounce into the puckerbrush or go into a jackknife, and if you saw a cop chasing an out-of-state motorist for speeding they both would be doing a courteous thirty-five. The Hudson was heavy enough to take the bumps, and still do a decent speed with cans secreted under the rear upholstery. My uncle's Hudson was the second-best automobile in town — the best was the Pierce-Arrow owned by Ike Skillin. We called it a Fierce-Sparrow and it was a handsome thing with fender lamps, but it was too fancy for the rigors of smuggling and probably couldn't have made a loaded escape over plowed ground. When my uncle asked me to take a ride I climbed right in.

On the face of it the errand was lawful. That year there was a big strike in the coal mines, and our little town faced a rough winter. It's a foolish man who freezes to death in a wooded country, but for the most part we had become coal burners. That year the farmers had sold all the spare dry wood they had, and the sawmill had moved all its slabs, but coal bins were empty all over town. My uncle stumbled on the news that during a strike certain import restrictions were relaxed, so he got all the retail coal dealers of Maine to join him in a bunch purchase of Russian anthracite. This was the day of the big meeting, and when he said, "Wanna go for a ride?" it was to this meeting we rode. It was my first view of any business transaction larger than a grocery order, and I am still amazed at the short time it took.

We didn't hit any sixty on the way. The Hudson purred along moderately and we came to the Portland waterfront. Portland still had a waterfront then, and there were vessels in the harbor and considerable activity. The Grand Trunk was bringing grain down from Saskatchewan and Manitoba, for one thing. The railroad was shifting cars around from dock to dock, and while there were a few trucks there were many teams. The only place that wasn't busy was the coal dock, and that's where we went. Up on the second floor, where they had a coal stove that was burning wood, we found the fuel dealers of Maine congregated. I stood over in the corner out of the way, and my uncle shook hands with all the coal men, bankers, ship brokers, insurance men, consular agents, customs officials and lawyers who had come together to arrange this momentous deal. Introductions and handshakes went on and on, and finally a big pile of papers was passed from man to man for signatures, and the deal was completed. They had bought Maine's coal for the next three years, and the miners in Pennsylvania could go hang! Then the handshaking went all the way around again, and my uncle and I came away.

When we got out on the wharf the Hudson was gone. I was upset by this, and thought my uncle was far too unconcerned. "I think somebody is gassing it up for me," he said. So we walked around a little, and watched a man taking an engine out of a pleasure boat, and before long the Hudson came loping down onto the pier and the man who was driving it seemed to know my uncle. "She's all ready to go," he said, and when my uncle paid him for the gasoline it seemed to me like a great deal of money. And the Hudson didn't seem to ride so well on the way home. Going up Custom House Hill my uncle had to drop into low gear. That's all I know.

When the first shipload of Russian coal arrived at Portland a couple of weeks later a lot of people had a lot of work to do. Every coal dealer in Maine got his proportionate share of the cargo, and began filling the orders that had backlogged. The railroad gondolas were spotted over the coal pockets on the spur track, and every half-wit in town, including me, was down there screening, bagging and loading coal. The regular crews were trotting the horses around to get at least some amount of coal in each empty bin, and our job was to keep them from waiting too long when they got back to the pockets. I'd go down for an hour after school every evening, and work all day on Saturday and Sunday. Nobody had thought up a mechanical loader, so we used the big coal scoops and shoveled. Five scoops made a cwt., subject to correction on the big beam platform scales up at the the office. Coal was coal then, and everybody took what the Russians sent — mostly it was the egg size. A few people came to my uncle and said, "I always have chestnut coal, you put egg coal in my bin!" My uncle would smile and give them a short account of the tight situation in the industry, which they always accepted, and then he'd chew the rest of the day about the stupid public. When the first shipment played out we had only to wait for the next vessel to arrive from Russia and then we began all over again.

The shoe shops in town never bought coal from my uncle but had it come directly from the mines by the carload, but that winter they came with their hats in their hands to see if he would take care of them. He liked that. They used to call him all kinds of names, to his face and behind it. Then he'd sit in his little office and chuckle.

There was still some traffic in cordwood then, and almost all the farmers sold some. But the up-to-date home was heated with coal, and we had a coal furnace in our cellar. It had two chains attached to the dampers, and these came upstairs so we had some control of the heat without going down cellar. But we still had to go down to throw on more coal, shake down the grate, clean out and sift the ashes and see that everything was right. Hot air flowed strictly by gravity — there was no blower — and appeared upstairs through registers in the floor of each room. At bedtime the furnace was shaken down and stoked, and after a few minutes for burning off the coal gas the chains would be set on "check" and we'd all retire. The furnace would stew along all night without making any great amount of heat, and the first person up in the morning would shift the chains. Now the draft was free, and presently a little warmth would begin to seep up through the registers. While Mother made breakfast we children would hover over the registers and brush up our homework, and she used to say the house would warm faster if we didn't soak up so much heat when it went by.

Sifting ashes was a dirty and unpleasant job, and we were glad to find that the Russian coal was free-burning and we didn't have to sift it. The ash sifter was a basketlike round container with a mesh bottom, and it fitted loosely into the top of a barrel. The ashes taken from the bottom of the furnace were put in the sifter, and we could thus reclaim clinkers and half-burnt coal so we could put them through the fire again and get our money's worth. By throwing a grain bag or old rug over the sifter you could hold down some of the dust, but it was still a dirty job. I can taste coal-ash dust in my throat now. Not long ago I saw an ash sifter in an antique shop, tossed into a corner with other junk, and the man didn't even know what it was.

Once or twice as we doled out the Russian coal I got a chance to ride with the teamsters and help put coal down cellar. We'd back the horses in, open a cellar window, and while a woman stood down there and told us to look out for her preserve shelves we'd stick in the long steel chutes. If the coal was in bags we'd dump it, and if 'twas loose we'd shovel. My job was to pick up any pieces of coal that hopped out of the chute and lay on the ground, or snow. Handling coal was a dirty, cold, miserable job that I hated all the way. Ice was some fun, but not coal. I think I, too, would have considered smuggling.

One by one furnaces were "converted" to oil; then one by one new oil-burning furnaces went in. Kitchen ranges were fitted with oil burners, with bottles hanging by them. You could always tell if a house burned oil in the range the instant you stepped through the door — it did something to the oxygen, and it always killed geraniums. "Don't understand it," a woman would say. "Never had any trouble with geraniums before." We heard talk of gun-types and wall-flames. There was a pot burner, and finally the sophisticated Heatrola. This was an ornate marriage of the parlor heater and the Victrola phonograph, except that it wouldn't play any music. Why a front-room stove should look like a gramophone is on the conscience of American technocracy. But one day the coal business followed the ice business, and my uncle became a full-time bootlegger.

They never caught him either.

THE SMALLEST HALL

WE had a picture house in our town — the Nordica Theatre. It was named to honor the sweet singer from Sandy River Valley, Mme. Lillian Nordica, but she never saw it and it was a dubious kind of honor. The place was owned and operated by Mrs. Mortimer, who sold tickets behind the glass wicket, couldn't spell, and had some special faculty for finding the worst movies. This was before block bookings and the theatre trust, and the films came by mail. Sometimes the crowd would assemble but the films wouldn't arrive, so Mrs. Mortimer would sadly refund our money. During the years I was a communicant at this shrine of culture I saw the rise and fall of the Walk-Over Shoe commercial.

We didn't know the word commercial in that sense, then, but that's what this was. The Walk-Over Shoe film at the Nordica was the first advertising film of the now-famous L. L. Bean, who at that time had the shoe, clothing and sporting goods store on our Main

Street in partnership with his brother Guy. It was called Bean's, but the sign over the store said *L. L. & G. C. Bean*. Amongst other things, they had the local dealership for the nice-nice Walk-Over Shoes—which were not made in our shoemaking town. L. L. outlived his brothers, all, but he and Guy were a lot alike in their courteous, chummy handling of customers. I would go in for my annual pair of Lion Brand boots and come out feeling that I had just enjoyed converse with the wise of all ages and was by far the most important person in the whole world. Even then L. L. was toying with his idea for a mail-order business, but this didn't impress anybody so much as his shooting gallery in the basement of his store. I'd be trying on my boots and the target shooting downstairs would sound like the Battle of Gettysburg. When one day I was invited to step down and shoot I thought I had arrived—but I knew I had when Dr. Gilchrist invited me to use his rifle.

The Walk-Over Shoe commercial was a short film cartoon that the Bean Brothers paid Mrs. Mortimer to run every night between the serial and the funny picture. When it first appeared it was sharp and smooth, clear and amusing. It showed a pirate ship which sailed in and dropped anchor. The longboat was lowered, and a half dozen fierce and eye-patched pirates with wooden legs came ashore and walked up the beach. There they dug a hole and uncovered a metal-bound sea chest of treasure-trove which they prized open. The treasure proved to be a beautiful pair of Walk-Over Shoes, and then the screen would say, *L. L. & G. C. Bean.*

But as the years ran along and the film scraped nightly through Mrs. Mortimer's pioneer projector, disintegration accumulated. Pieces would break out and she'd patch it. The cartoon got jumpy, and the celluloid was raked with scratches. It finally got down to an illegible light and shadow that fluttered and humped for about eight seconds, and then the screen would say, *L. L. & G. C. Bean.* Mrs. Mortimer would leave the firm name on the screen for the full time of the original cartoon, thus giving the Beans full value, but giving the rest of us some nausea. In after-years L. L. Bean was recalling this and he said, "We never sold very many."

We went to the Nordica "to the pictures." We didn't say movies then, and never heard of cinema and flicks. As soon as Mrs. Mortimer had a picture booked, even if it wouldn't come for six months, she would letter a glass slide to announce it. She always spelled *coming* with two *m*'s. Everybody in town knew better, except Mrs. Mortimer, and we'd applaud the word *Comming* so Mrs. Mortimer believed we were pleased at the picture she had selected. We had one schoolteacher who when a child missed a word in the spelling bee, would say, "All right, Mrs. Mortimer, you may sit down."

At first Mrs. Mortimer's picture house was also a dance hall. Couples who didn't like the picture, or for some other reason, could get up and dance in a dimly lit sidehall to the same music that was accompanying the pictures. Films were silent, and we watched them rather than listened to them. So the dancing didn't interfere too much with the show. But afterwards, for some reason, Mrs. Mortimer partitioned off the dance floor and converted the side-hall into a bowling alley. The bowling didn't bother the picture show much either, but once in a while we'd see a live stage show at the Nordica, and then the falling pins were objectionable.

The Nordica's stage was not designed for live shows. It had no dressing rooms, and the front velvet curtain pulled aside instead of going up and down. For picture shows this curtain remained closed while the audience assembled, and then Tushy Greenleaf, who took tickets, swept up, and ushered the elderly, would pass through the little door backstage, and everybody would clap hands when he drew the curtain back. This revealed the white-painted plaster screen. The usual program was a Pathé news, a cliff-hanger serial, a one-reel funny picture, the comming attractions, and the feature photoplay — not counting the Walk-Over cartoon. As soon as Tushy pulled the curtain the piano player would strike up "Hello, Everybody — Hello!" and then trail off into an evening of improvisations to suit a film she had never seen before. Playing piano for silent films was a special art, and wasn't easy. You had to be ready with the "Ride of the Valkyries" for the steeplechase, and shift to "Hearts and Flowers" for the kissing scenes. In the sad places you played sad music.

Limited as it was, we did use the Nordica stage

for plays, and for the annual Board of Trade minstrel show. The three-act farce of my senior year, *Ruth in a Rush,* was done the same night as the playoff in the town bowling league. At the climax of the second act, when Lloyd Towle came crawling over the blazing desert sands to cry, "We are lost!" Benny Stilkey got a strike on alley three and a great cheer went up. The biggest dramatic success of the year, in our town, was the Board of Trade minstrels, and they were always at the Nordica.

My recollection of these minstrels causes me to wonder now why the modern National Association for the Advancement of Colored People is so touchy about blackface comedy. I think, in our terms, they are making an intellectual error, as when highway engineers tear down historic wooden bridges. We didn't know what a Negro was in our town, with the single presumptive exception of the Murchisons. With them we weren't sure. Otherwise, we'd see a porter on the Pullmans of the Maritime Express, and at eighty miles an hour we didn't exactly get to know him. We had no attitudes one way or the other — we weren't informed and we didn't know.

But every minstrel show had four end men in blackface and instead of being some kind of a left-handed insult to the Negro it was the sincerest kind of tribute. These four men were our most talented local performers. Furthermore, it was never the Negro, or imitation Negro, who was the butt of the minstrel-show joke — but the interlocutor and the public, none of them black. The interlocutor was the Great Stuffed Shirt, in tails and top hat, and his remarks were stilted and stuffy. The end man was the big hero, the one to be remembered and quoted, and the one who got called back again and again for another chorus. There was absolutely nothing in our Down East minstrel shows that calls for such present-day concern by the NAACP — if people will take the time to understand.

But it was a hands-off libel of anybody and everybody else. The minstrel show had more immunity than a congressman on his way to the Capitol. After the opening chorus of plantation songs "by the entire company" Mr. Bones would be revealed in hysterics. His neighbor would thump him on the back, douse him with a pail of water, and restore him to his senses.

"Mr. Bones, what in the world transpired to throw you into this paroxysm of unbridled hilarity?" the interlocutor would say.

There would be more yuk-yukking, and Mr. Bones would say, "Mr. Interlocutor, do you know which am de smallest hall in town?"

Adjusting his silk hat, the interlocutor would appear to meditate, and then he would say, "Now, Mr. Bones, permit me to concentrate on the significance of the conundrum you have just propounded — I believe you asked which is the smallest hall in town?"

"Dat's right — which am de smallest hall in town?"

"Would it be the Knights of Pythias hall?"

"No, sir, Mr. Interlocutor, dat ain't it at all, no-how, yuk-yuk-yuk!"

"I wonder if it would be the Harraseeket Grange hall?"

"No, sir — dat ain't it . . ."

"How about the Masonic Hall?"

"No, it ain't de Masons' Hall."

"Well, then, Mr. Bones — I'm afraid I shall be obliged to confess that I am not well enough informed about our local architectural capacities to be able to designate which hall in town is the smallest. Which is the smallest hall in town?"

"You give up, Mr. Interlocutor?"

"Yes, Mr. Bones — I give up."

"Yuk-yuk! Well — de smallest hall in town am dat measly, stingy, penny-pinchin' hall, Mr. Reuben W. Hall!"

Interlocutor: "And now, ladies and gentlemen, that sterling portrayist of delightful harmony on the incomparable five-string banjo, Mr. Bones — in a rendition of his own composition entitled 'Feet, Dance Your Toes Off!' "

Always Mr. Reuben W. Hall, who got a "joke" every year, tried to look pleased at this free advertising, but his chief solace was that in the next joke somebody else would be slandered. One year Ray Dyer, who was portly and ran a tearoom, spent months and months composing verses to the tune of "How do you do, everybody, how do you do." Every verse was clearly actionable, and he had one for about everybody in town. He went on and on, and every time they called him back he'd have more. One verse, about Harry Merrill, who was fat, went this way:

How do you do, Harry Merrill,
  How do you do?
How do you do, Harry Merrill,
  How are you?

When you're sick and failing fast,
Will you operate or blast?
  How do you doodle, doodle,
    Doodle, doodle, doo!

But even in my boyhood the tendency was growing. It became unkind to play a "colored man," and the minstrel show went its way. They changed the name to variety show, kept everybody white, and some years called it just a vaudeville show — but it wasn't the same. One year there was no Board of Trade stage show, and that was that. The Nordica Theatre is still there, but it isn't the same, either. Mrs. Mortimer sold out to a new owner, and he spoiled everything by spelling *comming* with only one *m*.

THE PRAYER MEETING

O F all the days of the week Wednesday was the most sinful as far as I know. This was because of prayer meeting. I'm sure of the young ladies who were seduced before their time by far the most of them enjoyed it on the way home from prayer meeting. It was a matter of time, availability, and the low quality of ministerial intellect. Ministers didn't have any gimmicks, and they thought more people would turn out if the meeting didn't last too long. Most of us had a ten o'clock deadline, and we'd break away from sociables and dances, and such iniquitous fleshpot frivolities, at nine-forty-five, hand the young lady over to her parents, and still be home in time. But the Wednesday testimonial session would start at seven, finish before eight, and we'd have the evening to explore in all directions.

Our pleasures, with the possible exception of Wednesdays, were decorous and simple. It would be fun to jerk a spasm addict of the beatnik philosophy back to one of our vestry sociables and see what he thinks of it. We didn't dance, because nobody danced in a church vestry, but we played games and had refreshments at a total charge of ten cents. The ladies who sponsored the event would bring cakes, and the ten cents would pay for the cocoa and ice cream. The hot cocoa was made in a big tin kettle and always had a church-vestry burnt flavor. Whenever I drink cocoa I always think of a girl named Sarah-Anne, vaguely, because her mother always made the cocoa and Sarah-Anne dipped it.

The two dominant games of our vestry sociables were Winkum and Seven In and Seven Out. While somebody played "The Connecticut March" on the piano, couples would parade in a circle. Odd girls stood inside the circle and odd boys outside. The idea was to count off seven couples as they passed and then cut in. If the right girl didn't come along to make the precise count you could stand there going, "Six, six, six, six, six . . ." until she did. In Winkum the girls sat in chairs in a circle, and the boys partnered behind them. One boy had an empty chair, and he was expected to wink some girl over to him.

She would try to go, but her partner would restrain her with his hands on her shoulders. If she succeeded in leaving, then her vacant place was to be filled the same way. A very gay game. In extreme exuberance, when he had some girl he wanted to keep, a boy could wind up on the floor with a half nelson around his prize, restraining her while he kicked the chair into a corner and the chaperones shouted, "Not so rough!" This close contact of the sexes, at a sedate vestry sociable, gained some dignity in the surroundings, and could be explored further on the way home.

There is one definite and honest thing I can say about our childhood parties — there was no liquor. No matter how the historians record the prohibition days, we had no flasks and we never tasted bathtub gin. The closest we ever came to booze was in school when we had the annual Frances E. Willard program. Frances E. Willard was a temperance reformer who organized the Women's Christian Temperance Union, and years ago her followers succeeded in getting the Maine legislature to insist on abstinence advice in the public curriculum. This boiled down to one day a year when one of the Fellows sisters would show up and read us a canned lecture from national headquarters. It was the same lecture every year, and it included the demonstration that a worm will die if you drop him in whiskey. In high school we learned in the laboratory that anything will die if you drop it in whiskey, but in the lower grades this was an effective demonstration. The dying worm was a convincing sight. One time George Hunter raised his hand and inquired of Miss Fellows where she had obtained the whiskey in which she killed the worm — she being a W.C.T.U. officer and Maine being dry. Another time after a Frances E. Willard Day, John Goodey came to school and made a big stink with the teachers — he said his children came home and dug up a lot of worms and put them in his whiskey bottle, and if this happened again he'd burn the school down. I remember another father who made a lot of talk about it — he liked a snort now and then, and he resented the school's teaching his boy to call him a drunkard. But we got Frances E. Willard once a year, and as youngsters growing up we knew little else about spirits.

Some of our best parties came in winter at the one-room schools. The school bus hadn't been invented then and the centralized school was ahead of us. Each district of the town had its rural school, and out of school hours they were available. So in the winter a hayrack loaded with men, women and children would start out for one of these schools, and somebody would have gone on ahead with a sleigh to start the oyster stew and push back the desks. Some of those schools were heated by tall station-agent stoves, and the stew had to be made from a chair or stepladder. When the hayrack pulled up in a peal of bells, the runners creaking on the snow, and we climbed down to go into the school, the smell of an oyster stew in the making was about as nice as anything you could fit a nostril to. Also, an oyster stew on a cold night is a sweat-maker, and

I discovered at these parties that the lady who sweats the most is often the best dancer. I'm sure a modern twistomaniac, gyrating madly with a skinny female in frenzy, rich in his own sense of importance, thinks he has something. He doesn't have any idea. Take a rumpy mother of about fifty, gay at being out of the house for an evening, slog her full of three bowls of oyster stew, start the fiddles for a "Hull's Victory," and you've got something worth dancing with. These are the ones who swing you out of your shoes. Light as a feather on their feet, they love to dance. You never get to hold their hands — they always have a wet handkerchief and you don't mind. The other hand, around her ample waist, feels the corset stays bend and fret — somehow inside her gear she manages to convey uninhibited abandon. When the caller shouts, "Ladies chain!" you want to be ready. The debutantes of our time made nice friends and sweethearts, but an oyster stew time gave their mothers a chance to shine. Junie's mother, Mrs. Tidish, said to me once, "Why do you always pick me, can't you dance sometimes with Junie?" I told her I'd wait for Junie to learn to dance like her mother. Junie always hated me, but Mrs. Tidish danced with me any time I asked her. I'd find her over by the open door, pulling out the front of her dress to let a little air in, panting, and swabbing at her neck with a wet handkerchief. She was plump.

At church sociables we had a piano. At schoolhouse parties we would add a violin. A three-piece orchestra was high class. Once the Knights of Pythias held a Ladies' Night and brought on a five-piece orchestra from Portland, with a drummer, and a lot of people who didn't care for parties just went to hear it play. Many times there was no ticket charge, but a passed hat would raise enough — the piano player was only a dollar. I always had ten cents to drop in. When I'd ride up on the seat alongside Secretary Potter, three miles out to the Pleasant View School, hear all the wonderful singing in the hayrack behind me, enjoy an oyster stew and dance all evening, I'd drop my dime in the hat without stint — for it was worth it, every cent.

Come to think of it — I used to drop a dime in the Wednesday night prayer-meeting collection, too.

THE PARTING SHOT

THERE is a patent test used in our schools today to ascertain the intelligence of our modern boyhood, and girlhood. Teachers all over the country have used it for the past four or five years. One section asks the youngster to "match up" certain things that "go together." For instance, he finds a picture of a horse, and then a picture of a wagon. He is supposed to match up the horse and wagon. The horse and wagon go together. If the youngster does not put the horse with the wagon he is stupid.

There is one smallish fault with this test — probably unimportant in this day and age. There is only one horse shown, but the wagon is equipped with a pole for double harness.

Except for the professional half-wits, Secretary Potter was about as dumb as anybody we had in our town. If he could take this big, modern, computer-machine test in one of our bright-shining schools today, I could prove this assessment of Potter's mentality — because he would never have tried to insert an unmarried horse into a double harness.

Is there not something about this that merits our serious contemplation?

HUMOR | MEMOIR $16.95

There used to be a time when marvelous skyrockets could be purchased for a dime and the iceman came around once a week, when throwing a cap on and off took special talent and pants had watch pockets. When John Gould was young, it didn't take much to amuse a boy. He would wake up in the morning ready to be "amazed all day long at all manner of things."

Warmth, humor, nostalgia—these pages are filled with them, all conveyed lovingly in John Gould's signature wit. This book is for anyone who has ever been young and wants to remember or who just wants to laugh with Gould as he recounts his experiences growing up in another era.

Born and bred in Maine, JOHN GOULD (1908–2003) was well known for his acerbic Yankee wit. Over the course of his life he wrote dozens of books and for an astounding sixty-two years was a regular columnist for the *Christian Science Monitor*. Despite his literary fame, he steadfastly claimed that he was first, last, and always a farmer.

Down East Books
An imprint of Rowman & Littlefield
800-462-6420 | www.rowman.com

Distributed by
NATIONAL BOOK NETWORK

ISBN 978-1-60893-550-5
51695
9 781608 935505

Cover photo: © Dave Reede/GettyImages
Cover design by Neil Cotterill